More musical knights

Harty Mackerras
Rattle Pritchard

Discographies compiled
by John Hunt

CONTENTS

3	Acknowledgement
4	Introduction
5	Hamilton Harty
71	Charles Mackerras
203	Simon Rattle
259	John Pritchard
345	Credits

More Musical Knights
Published by John Hunt.
Designed by Richard Chluparty
© 1997 John Hunt
reprinted 2009
ISBN 978-1-901395-03-7

Sole distributors:
Travis & Emery,
17 Cecil Court,
London, WC2N 4EZ,
United Kingdom.
(+44) 20 7 459 2129.
sales@travis-and-emery.com

ACKNOWLEDGEMENT

These publications have been made possible by contributions and advance subscriptions from the following:

Masakasu Abe, Chiba
Richard Ames, New Barnet
Stefano Angeloni, Frasso Sabino
Stathis Arfanis, Athens
Yoshihiro Asada, Osaka
Jack Atkinson, Tasmania
Eduardo Chibas, Caracas
Robert Christoforides, Fordingbridge
F. De Vilder, Bussum
Richard Dennis, Greenhithe
John Derry, Newcastle-upon-Tyne
Hans-Peter Ebner, Milan
Henry Fogel, Chicago
Peter Fu, Hong Kong
Nobuo Fukumoto, Hamamatsu
Peter Fulop, Toronto
James Giles, Sidcup
Jens Golumbus, Hamburg
Jean-Pierre Goossens, Luxembourg
Gordon Grant, Seattle
Johann Gratz, Vienna
Michael Harris, London
Tadashi Hasegawa, Nagoya
Naoya Hirabayashi, Tokyo
Donald Hodgman, Riverside CN
Martin Holland, Sale
Bodo Igesz, New York
Richard Igler, Vienna

Shiro Kawai, Tokyo
Andrew Keener, New Malden
Detlef Kissmann, Solingen
Elisabeth Legge-Schwarzkopf DBE, Zürich
John Mallinson, Hurst Green
Carlo Marinelli, Rome
Finn Moeller Larsen, Virum
Philip Moores, Stafford
Bruce Morrison, Gillingham
W. Moyle, Ombersley
Alan Newcombe, Hamburg
Hugh Palmer, Chelmsford
Jim Parsons, Sutton Coldfield
Laurence Pateman, London
James Pearson, Vienna
Johann Christian Petersen, Hamburg
Tully Potter, Billericay
Patrick Russell, Calstock
Yves Saillard, Mollie-Margot
Neville Sumpter, Northolt
Yoshihiko Suzuki, Tokyo
H.A. Van Dijk, Apeldoorn
Mario Vicentini, Cassano Magnago
Hiromitsu Wada, Chiba
Urs Weber, St Gallen
Nigel Wood, London
G. Wright, Romford

MORE MUSICAL KNIGHTS

Like the first volume of British conductors which I compiled in 1995, this group spans the earliest days of recording from around 1909 (Sir Hamilton Harty) to include two practitioners still active in the commercial recording studios (Sir Charles Mackerras and Sir Simon Rattle). In the latter cases, of course, it is very much a matter of work still in progress.

To the above mentioned I have added the much-undervalued Sir John Pritchard, the first British music director of Glyndebourne Festival Opera and subsequently an ambassador for British music-making on the international opera scene. His services for Mozart started with early Philips LPs for the 1956 bi-centenary celebrations to 1980s Decca recordings of "Idomeneo" and "Der Schauspieldirektor" with the Vienna Philharmonic, versions refreshingly without concessions to period practice.

In the cases both of Pritchard and Mackerras, their high repute as operatic accompanists is confirmed by countless recital LPs and CDs, in which they are heard working with eminent singers from the golden age (Schwarzkopf and Jurinac) to more modern divas (Cotrubas, Kanawa, Mattila, Fleming).

Harty, the earliest of Berlioz specialists and a fine advocate of British music of his time (Lambert and Walton), is heard also as chamber musician and piano accompanist - although it has not proved possible to date accurately all of his earliest recordings in the latter capacity.

I would not wish to imply that the only British conductors worth chronicling are those who have been decorated with a knighthood. In fact in my view there are some who hold such a title whose work does not deserve to be taken too seriously - but that is another matter!

It is hoped that these discographies will emphasise the diversity and quality of British music-making. There are some musicians who, through their very versatility, suffer when assessments are made, as if diversification in itself were some sort of weakness.

The 3-column layout continues to be used for these discographies, which are arranged alphabetically by composer. Information in the first column indicates the city or suburb where the recording took place, followed now by a precise date wherever possible (day, month, year). Where a recording was spread over a period of time, only the first and last dates are given, but this does not always imply that sessions took place on all intervening days. Second column indicates lists other artists taking part, such as singers, instrumentalists and orchestras, or if the conductor is acting in the capacity of piano accompanist. The only abbreviations are for orchestras (LPO, LSO and RPO for London orchestras, CBSO for City of Birmingham, VPO and VSO for Vienna). The third column of the discography attempts to list as many catalogue numbers as possible for the main territories and for the principal formats of 78, EP (45), LP and CD (cassette tapes are not normally included). Information may not be copmplete for all overseas areas and I am always glad to hear from collectors who can add numbers or point out possible errors. Catalogue numbers which appear on the same line of text, usually separated by "/", often indicate the simultaneous mono and stereo editions of an LP which became customary in the 1950s and 1960s. For example, HMV had ALP (mono) and ASD (stereo), Columbia 33CX (mono) and SAX (stereo) and Decca LXT (mono) and SXL (stereo). It should also be borne in mind that some catalogue numbers may be for sets in which the work in question is grouped together with other pieces.

Hamilton Harty
1879-1941

Discography compiled by John Hunt

JOHANN SEBASTIAN BACH (1685-1750)

Orchestral Suite No 2

London 20 January 1924	Orchestra Murchie, flute	Columbia L 1557-1558 Columbia (USA) M 13

Air (Orchestral Suite No 3)

London 20 January 1924	Orchestra	Columbia 980 Columbia (USA) M 13

Concerto in D minor for 2 violins and orchestra

London 10 April 1924	Orchestra Catterall, Bridge	Columbia L 1613-1615 Columbia (USA) M 13

MILY BALAKIREV (1837-1910)

Russia, Second overture on Russian themes

London   LPO   Columbia DB 1236-1237
12 September   Columbia (USA) 7031-7032D
1933   CD: Dutton CDAX 8005
                                  <u>Original issue formed part of Columbia's</u>
                                  <u>History of Music series</u>

HUBERT BATH (1883-1945)

Sunset on the Veldt for cello and piano

London   Squire   Columbia L 1042
1916   Harty, piano

ARNOLD BAX (1883-1953)

Overture to a Picaresque comedy

London   LPO   Columbia LX 394
15 April   CD: Dutton CDLX 7016
1935

LUDWIG VAN BEETHOVEN (1770-1827)

Symphony No 4

Manchester 26-27 November 1926	Hallé	Columbia L 1875-1879 Columbia (USA) M 47 Columbia (Japan) 4 LP: Columbia (USA) RL 3034

Piano Concerto No 3

London 6 April 1925	Orchestra Murdoch	Columbia l 1686-1689

Romance No 1 for violin and orchestra

London 1919	Orchestra D.Kennedy	Columbia L 1340

Die Ehre Gottes aus der Natur/Gellert Lieder, arrangement

London 29 August 1922	Orchestra Butt Sung in English	Columbia 7265

In questa tomba oscura

London 30 August 1922	Orchestra Butt	Columbia 7267

HECTOR BERLIOZ (1803-1869)

Béatrice et Bénédict, overture

London 9 November 1934	LPO	Columbia LX 371 Columbia (USA) 68342D LP: World Records SH 148 CD: Pearl GEMMCD 9485

Le carnaval romain, overture

Manchester 29 October 1924	Hallé	Columbia L 1650 Columbia (USA) 67087D
Manchester 18 February 1932	Hallé	Columbia LX 291 Columbia (France) DFX 117 Columbia (USA) 68221D Columbia (Japan) J 8075 LP: World Records SH 148 CD: Pearl GEMMCD 9485

Le corsair, overture

London 9 November 1934	LPO	Columbia DX 644 Columbia (USA) 68287D LP: World Records SH 148 CD: Pearl GEMMCD 9485

La damnation de Faust, Marche hongroise

Manchester 13 December 1920	Hallé	Columbia L 1405
Manchester 2 May 1927	Hallé	Columbia L 2069 Columbia (USA) 50086D/7188MA Columbia (Japan) J 7331 CD: Pearl GEMMCD 9485

La damnation de Faust, Danse des sylphes

Manchester 2 May 1927	Hallé	Columbia L 2069 Columbia (USA) 50086D/7188MA Columbia (Japan) J 7331 CD: Pearl GEMMCD 9485

Funeral march from last scene of Tristia

London 15 April 1935	LPO	Columbia LX 421 Columbia (USA) 68429D LP: World Records SH 148 CD: Pearl GEMMCD 9485 CD: Dutton CDLX 7016 SH 148 dated 26 April

Roméo et Juliette, Queen Mab scherzo

Manchester 2 May 1927	Hallé	Columbia L 1989 Columbia (USA) 67422D CD: Pearl GEMMCD 9485

Roméo et Juliette, Roméo seul et fête des Capulets

London 5-9 September 1933	LPO L.Goossens	Columbia DB 1230-1231 LP: World Records SH 148 CD: Pearl GEMMCD 9485 CD: Dutton CDLX 7016 Original issue formed part of Columbia's History of Music series

Le roi Lear, overture

London 16 October 1935	LSO	Decca K 792-793 Decca (USA) 25339-25340

Les troyens, Marche troyenne

London	LSO	Decca K 793
16 October		Decca (USA) 25340
1935		CD: Pearl GEMMCD 9485

Les troyens, Royal Hunt and Storm

London	Hallé	Columbia DX 291
10 April		Columbia (France) DFX 117
1931		Columbia (USA) 68043D
		Columbia (Japan) J 7986
		CD: Pearl GEMMCD 9485

HENRY BISHOP (1786-1855)

Home sweet home

London 23 March 1921	Orchestra Stralia	Columbia 7262

GEORGES BIZET (1838-1875)

Carmen, excerpt (La fleur que tu m'avais jetée)

London 23 June 1926	Orchestra Lindi	Columbia L 1816 <u>Later recording of same aria with same catalogue number but not conducted by Harty</u>

Carmen, excerpt (Je dis que rien ne m'épouvante)

London 5 May 1920	Orchestra Stralia <u>Sung in English</u>	Columbia 7247
London 31 December 1924	Orchestra Stralia <u>Sung in English</u>	Columbia 7332 <u>Previous recording of same aria with same catalogue number but not conducted by Harty</u>

Carmen, excerpt (Parle-moi de ma mère)

London 24 October 1924	Orchestra Licette, Mullings <u>Sung in English</u>	Columbia L 1664

LUIGI BOCCHERINI (1743-1805)

Rondo, arranged for cello and piano by Squire

London 1916	Squire Harty, piano	Columbia L 1032

JOHANNES BRAHMS (1833-1897)

Violin Concerto

Manchester 3-5 December 1928	Hallé Szigeti	Columbia L 2265-2269 Columbia (USA) M 117 Columbia (Japan) 74 LP: Columbia (USA) M6X 31513 CD: Pearl GEMMCD 9345 CD: EMI CDH 566 4212

Academic Festival Overture

Manchester 29 October 1924	Hallé	Columbia L 1637 Columbia (USA) 67085D

Hungarian Dances nos. 5 and 6

Manchester Date not confirmed	Hallé	Columbia 5466 Columbia (USA) 2020D/2083M Columbia (Japan) J 5090 CD; Avid Records AMSC 577

Hungarian Dances nos 2 and 7, arranged for violin and piano by Joachim

Details not confirmed	I.Menges Harty, piano	Details not confirmed

Clarinet Trio in A minor

London	Draper,	Columbia L 1609-1611
21 October	Squire,	Columbia (USA) M 19
1924	Harty, piano	

Scherzo in C minor "Sonatensatz"

London	D.Kennedy	Columbia L 1337
1919	Harty, piano	

Adagio from Violin Sonata no 3, abridged

London	D.Kennedy	Columbia L 1337
1919	Harty, piano	

MAX BRUCH (1838-1920)

Violin Concerto No 1

London 9 April 1925	Orchestra Sammons	Columbia L 1680-1682 Columbia (USA) M 30

CHARLES CADMAN (1881-1946)

At dawning

London 27 February 1926	Baillie Harty, piano	LP: EMI HLM 7064/RLS 714/ 1C 177 05783-05784M <u>Test recording not published in 78rpm format</u>

FREDERIC CHOPIN (1810-1849)

Mazurka, arranged for cello and piano by Squire

Details not confirmed	Squire Harty, piano	Columbia D 1334

Nocturne in E flat, arranged for cello and piano by Squire

Details not confirmed	Squire Harty, piano	Columbia D 1425

Nocturne in E, arranged for violin and piano by Auer

Details not confirmed	I.Menges Harty, piano	Columbia D 355

JEREMIAH CLARKE (1674-1707)

Trumpet Voluntary, previously attributed to Purcell

Manchester 2 May 1927	Hallé Harris	Columbia L 1986 Columbia (USA) 7136M Columbia (Japan) J 7189 LP: EMI MRS 5141/1C 047 05161M

FREDERICK CLAY (1838-1889)

I'll sing thee songs of Araby

London 25 February 1920	Eisdell Harty, piano	Columbia L 1369 <u>Same catalogue number also used for versions of this song with a different pianist</u>

FREDERIC COWEN (1852-1935)

The better land

London 23 March 1921	Orchestra Butt	Columbia 7260

CESAR CUI (1835-1918)

Orientale for cello and piano

Details not confirmed	Squire Harty, piano	Columbia D 1369

18 Harty

HART PEASE DANKS (1834-1903)

Silver threads among the gold, song arranged for cello and piano

London 1915	Squire Harty, piano	Columbia L 1003 Columbia (USA) A5832/7068M
London 30 August 1922	Squire Harty, piano	Columbia L 1003 <u>Second version</u>

CLAUDE DEBUSSY (1862-1918)

Prélude à l'après-midi d'un faune, abridged

Manchester 13 December 1920	Hallé	Columbia L 1405 Columbia (USA) 67053D

Minuet from Petite suite, arranged for cello and piano

Details not confirmed	Squire Harty, piano	Columbia D 1434

GAETONO DONIZETTI (1797-1848)

L'elisir d'amore, excerpt (Una furtiva lagrima)

London	Orchestra	Columbia L 1832
24 June	Hackett	
1926	Sung in English	

DUNKLER

Humoresque, arranged for cello and piano by Squire

London	Squire	Columbia L 1201
1917	Harty, piano	2 differing takes used

Rêverie for cello and piano

London	Squire	Columbia L 1233
1917	Harty, piano	
London	Squire	Columbia L 1233
30 August	Harty, piano	Second version
1922		

ANTONIN DVORAK (1841-1904)

Symphony No 9 "From the New World"

Manchester 10 April- 24 October 1923	Hallé	Columbia L 1523-1527 Columbia (USA) M 3
Manchester 2 May 1927	Hallé	Columbia L 1523R-1547R/9770-9774 Columbia (USA) M 77 Columbia (Japan) 36

Carnival overture, abridged

Manchester 2 May 1927	Hallé	Columbia L 2036 Columbia (USA) 67412D Columbia (Japan) J 7251

Slavonic Dance no 1, arranged for two pianos

Date not confirmed	Hess, Harty	Columbia DB 1235/(USA) M 334 CD; Pearl GEMMCD 9462 <u>Issued as part of Columbia's History of Music series</u>

HENRY ECCLES (1675-1735)

Sonata, arranged for cello and piano by Harty and Squire

London 1916	Squire Harty, piano	Columbia L 1053

EDWARD ELGAR (1857-1934)

Cello Concerto

Manchester 30 November 1930	Hallé Squire	Columbia DX 117-120 Columbia (USA) M 247 Columbia (Japan) 175 LP: Imprimatur IMP 1

Enigma Variations

London March 1932	Hallé	Columbia DX 322-325/8091-8094 Columbia (USA) M 165 LP: Imprimatur IMP 1 LP: BBC Records REH 756 CD: BBC Records BBCCD 756

Dream children

London March 1932	Hallé	Columbia DX 325 Columbia (USA) M 165 LP: BBC Records REH 756 CD: BBC Records BBCCD 756

The Apostles, excerpt (By the wayside)

Manchester 21 January 1927	Hallé Orchestra and Choir Labbette, H.Williams, Noble, Eisdell, Easton	Columbia L 1968/9343 CD: Dutton CDAX 8019

Where corals lie/Sea Pictures

London 16 September 1920	Orchestra Butt	Columbia 7246

Rosemary, arranged for cello and piano

London 1916	Squire Harty, piano	Columbia L 1117

Royal Choral Society

Patron - - - HIS MAJESTY THE KING
President - H.R.H. THE DUKE OF CONNAUGHT, K.G.

FIFTY-FIFTH SEASON.   1925-1926.

ROYAL ALBERT HALL

Saturday Afternoon, February 27th, 1926, at 2.30
DOORS OPEN AT 1.30

THE DREAM OF
GERONTIUS
(ELGAR).

MISS MARGARET BALFOUR

MR. STEUART WILSON

MR. KENNETH ELLIS

At the Organ - - Mr. R. ARNOLD GREIR

THE ROYAL ALBERT HALL ORCHESTRA

Conductor - **SIR HAMILTON HARTY**

NEW RECORDS

Sir **HAMILTON HARTY** and the **HALLÉ ORCHESTRA**

ELECTRIC RECORDING

WONDERFUL CONCERT HALL RECORDS OF TRUMPET VOLUNTARY and SOLEMN MELODY

Columbia *New process* **RECORDS**

SEPTEMBER 1927

ESPOSITO

Irish suite, nos. 2, 3 and 5

Manchester 20 April 1922	Hallé	Columbia L 1434

GABRIEL FAURE (1845-1924)

Romance sans paroles, arranged for cello and piano

Date not confirmed	Squire Harty, piano	Columbia D 1377

JOHN FOULDS (1880-1939)

Canadian Boat Song for cello and piano

London 1916	Squire Harty, piano	Columbia L 1042

GABRIEL-MARIE (1852-1928)

La cinquantaine for cello and piano

London 1912	Squire Harty, piano	Columbia 7887/E 149
London 1915	Squire Harty, piano	Columbia D 1325

NIELS GADE (1817-1890)

2 Noveletten

Date not confirmed	Squire Harty, piano	Details not confirmed

EDWARD GERMAN (1862-1936)

Waltz Song (Tom Jones)

London 31 December 1924	Orchestra Stralia	Columbia 7323 <u>Previous recording with same catalogue number but not conducted by Harty</u>

ERNEST GILLET (1856-1940)

Passepied for cello and piano

Date not confirmed	Squire Harty, piano	Columbia D 1327

UMBERTO GIORDANO (1867-1948)

Andrea Chenier, excerpt (Nemico della patria)

London 1 September 1927	Orchestra Formichi	Columbia L 2065

ALEXANDER GLAZUNOV (1865-1936)

Sérénade espagnole for cello and piano

London	Squire	Columbia L 1117
1916	Harty, piano	

BENJAMIN GODARD (1849-1895)

Berceuse de Jocelyn, arranged for cello and piano

London	Squire	Columbia L 1007
1915	Harty, piano	

Staccato valse/6 morceaux pour violon et piano

London	I.Menges	Columbia 7925
1915	Harty, piano	CD: Appian APR 7015

EUGENE GOOSSENS (1893-1962)

Old Chinese folksong for cello and piano

Date not	Squire	Columbia D 1377
confirmed	Harty, piano	

FRANCOIS-JOSEPH GOSSEC (1734-1829)

Tambourin, arranged for cello and piano

Date not	Squire	Columbia D 1329
confirmed	Harty, piano	

CHARLES GOUNOD (1818-1893)

Faust, excerpt (Ah je ris!)

London	Orchestra	Columbia 7330
31 December	Stralia	Previous recording with same catalogue
1924	Sung in English	number but not conducted by Harty

Faust, excerpt (Vous qui faites l'endormie)

London	Orchestra	Columbia 747
1919	Allin	
	Sung in English	

Faust, excerpt (Salut demeure)

London	Orchestra	Columbia L 1789
17 February	Martin	
1926		

London	Orchestra	Columbia L 1832
25 June	Hackett	
1926	Sung in English	

La reine de Saba, excerpt (She alone charmeth)

London	Orchestra	Columbia 756
1924	Allin	Previous recording with same catalogue
	Sung in English	number but not conducted by Harty

Roméo et Juliette, excerpt (Je veux vivre dans cette rêve)

London	Orchestra	Columbia L 1665
14 January	Licette	
1925		

EDVARD GRIEG (1843-1907)

Violin Sonata in G, Allegretto and allegro animato only

London	D.Kennedy	Columbia L 1336
1919	Harty, piano	

Violin Sonata in F, Allegro con brio and allegro molto only

London	D.Kennedy	Columbia L 1440
23 June	Harty, piano	
1922		

REYNALDO HAHN (1875-1947)

Si mes vers avaient des ailes, song arranged for cello and piano

Date not	Squire	Columbia D 1334
confirmed	Harty, piano	

GEORGE FRIDERIC HANDEL (1685-1759)

Music for the Royal fireworks, suite arranged by Harty

London 15 April 1935	LPO	Columbia LX 389-390 Columbia (USA) M 229/X 51 LP: Columbia (USA) RL 3019 CD: Dutton CDLX 7016

Water Music suite, arranged by Harty

London 13 December 1920	Orchestra	Columbia L 1404 This record, containing 1st and 3rd parts of the suite, was not published: second part of the recording was not allocated a catalogue number
Manchester 10 October 1921- 20 April 1922	Hallé	Columbia L 1437-1438 Columbia (USA) 50003-50004D Catalogue numbers L 1437-1438 had been previously allocated to an unpublished recording of Schubert's A minor string quartet by the London String Quartet
London 14 May 1933	LPO	Columbia DX 538-539 Columbia (USA) X 13 LP: Columbia (USA) RL 3019 CD: Dutton CDLX 7016

Suite of movements from various Concerti grossi and the operas Ariodante and Rodrigo, arranged by Harty

Decca 15 October 1935	LSO	Decca K 795-796/AK 795-796 Decca (USA) 25610-25611

Organ Concerto in D, arranged by Harty

London 12 March 1934	LSO Dawber	Columbia LX 341 Columbia (USA) 68256D Odeon O-9412 <u>This recording may include discarded movements from an earlier arrangement of the Fireworks music</u>

Minuet, arranged for cello and piano by Squire

Date not confirmed	Squire Harty, piano	Columbia D 1391

Larghetto, arranged for cello and piano by Squire

Date not confirmed	Squire Harty, piano	Columbia D 1354

Minuet in F, arranged for violin and piano by Harty

Date not confirmed	T.Menges Harty, piano	Details not confirmed

Jephta, excerpt (Deeper and deeper still)

London 5 May 1919	Orchestra Mullings	Columbia L 1344

Partenope, excerpt (Hark the tempest wildly raging!)

London 30 April 1924	Orchestra Allin	Columbia L 1612

Semele, excerpt (Where'er you walk)

London 5 May 1919	Orchestra Mullings	Columbia L 1344

Serse, excerpt (Ombra mai fu)

Date not confirmed	Sharpe Harty, organ	Columbia D 436

Serse, Ombra mai fu arranged for cello and piano

London 1917	Squire Harty, piano	Columbia L 1201 <u>2 differing takes used</u>

HAMILTON HARTY (1879-1941)

Scherzo (An Irish Symphony)

Manchester 24 June 1929	Hallé	Columbia 9891 Columbia (Japan) J 7556 LP: BBC Records REH 756 CD: BBC Records BBCCD 756

Fantasy scenes from an Eastern romance

London 1919	Orchestra	Columbia 753-754

With the wild geese, symphonic poem

Manchester 26 March 1926	Hallé	Columbia L 1822-1823 LP: Pearl OPAL 801

FRANZ JOSEF HAYDN (1732-1809)

Symphony No 95

London 14-15 October 1935	LSO	Decca K 798-799 Decca (USA) 25598-25599

Symphony No 101 "Clock"

Manchester 2 May 1927	Hallé	Columbia L 2088-2091 Columbia (USA) M 76 Columbia (Japan) 35

Andante in E flat, arranged for cello and piano

London 1916	Squire Harty, piano	Columbia L 1032

ENGELBERT HUMPERDINCK (1854-1921)

Hänsel und Gretel, Dance duet arranged for chorus

Manchester	Hallé	Columbia 9909
24 June	Manchester	45: Columbia SEG 7705/SCD 2092
1929	Childrens Choir	LP: EMI MRS 5185/1C 047 01632M
		CD: Beulah 1PD 4

ADOLF JENSEN (1837-1879)

Murmelndes Lüftchen, song arranged for cello and piano

London	Squire	Columbia L 1100
1916	Harty, piano	

EDOUARD LALO (1823-1892)

Symphonie espagnole pour violon et orchestre

London	Orchestra	Columbia (USA) M 14
18 July	Strockoff	Not published in UK
1924		

CONSTANT LAMBERT (1905-1951)

The Rio Grande

London	Hallé	Columbia L 2373-2374
11 January	St Michael	Columbia (USA) X 52
1930	Singers	LP: World Records SH 227
	Whitehead	LP: BBC Records REH 756
	Harty, piano	CD: BBC Records BBCCD 756
	Lambert, conductor	

EDWIN LEMARE (1865-1934)

Andantino, arranged for cello and piano by Squire

London 1917	Squire Harty, piano	Columbia L 1233
London 30 August 1922	Squire Harty, piano	Columbia L 1233 <u>Second version</u>

RUGGERO LEONCAVALLO (1858-1919)

I pagliacci, excerpt (Si può?)

London 1 September 1927	Orchestra Formichi	Columbia D 1487 Columbia (USA) 2034M

ANATOLE LIADOV (1855-1914)

Musical snuffbox

London 1924	Orchestra	Columbia 980 Columbia (USA) 67096D

SAMUEL LIDDLE (1867-1951)

Abide with me

London 31 August 1922	Orchestra Butt	Columbia 7101 <u>Previous recordings of the song using same catalogue number but not conducted by Harty</u>

FRANZ LISZT (1811-1886)

Hungarian Rhapsody no 2

Manchester 10 April 1931	Hallé	Columbia LX 132 Columbia (USA) 50310D/7243M Columbia (Japan) J 7865

HAMISH MACCUNN (1868-1916)

Amourette

Date not confirmed	Harty, piano	Columbia D 1347

PIETRO MASCAGNI (1863-1945)

Cavalleria rusticana, excerpt (Voi lo sapete)

London 8 January 1925	Orchestra Stralia Sung in English	Columbia 7330 Previous recording of the aria with same catalogue number but not conducted by Harty

Cavalleria rusticana, excerpt (Tu qui Santuzza?)

London 5 May 1920	Orchestra Stralia, Mullings Sung in English	Columbia 7242/7333

JULES MASSENET (1842-1912)

Le jongleur de Notre Dame, excerpt (La sauge est en effet précieuse)

London	Orchestra	Columbia D 1491
1 September	Formichi	Columbia (USA) 2030M
1927		

NICHOLAS MEHUL (1763-1817)

Gavotte for cello and piano

| Date not | Squire | Columbia D 1347 |
| confirmed | Harty, piano | |

FELIX MENDELSSOHN-BARTHOLDY (1809-1847)

Symphony No 4 "Italian"

Manchester	Hallé	Columbia DX 342-344/DX 8095-8097
9 April		Columbia (USA) M 167
1931		Columbia (Japan) 138
		LP: Columbia (USA) RL 3033
		RL 3033 may not have been issued

GIACOMO MEYERBEER (1791-1864)

L'africaine, excerpt (O paradis!)

London 25 July 1925	Orchestra Hackett	Columbia 7271/7366
London 21 June 1926	Orchestra O'Sullivan	Columbia L 1828
London 1926	Orchestra Nash <u>Sung in English</u>	Columbia 9104

GRAHAM MOORE (1859-1916)

The blind boy, for cello and piano

| Date not
confirmed | Squire
Harty, piano | Columbia D 1337 |

WOLFGANG AMADEUS MOZART (1756-1791)

Symphony No 35 "Haffner"

Manchester	Hallé	Columbia L 1783-1785
23 March		Columbia (USA) M 42
1926		

Bassoon Concerto

London	Orchestra	Columbia L 1824-1826
30 March	Camden	Columbia (USA) M 71
1926		

Violin Concerto No 5

London	Orchestra	Columbia L 1592-1595
10 April	Catterall	Columbia (USA) M 11
1924		

Sinfonia concertante for violin, viola and orchestra

London	LPO	Columbia DX 478-481/DX 8041-8044
30 April	Sammons, Tertis	Columbia (USA) M 188
1933		LP: EMI HQM 1055
		CD: Biddulph LAB 023

Divertimento No 17, movements 1-3 and 6

London 17 October 1934	LPO	Columbia LX 350-352/DX 8132-8134 Columbia (USA) M 207/MM 207

Violin Sonata No 34 K526

London 27 April 1923	Catterall Harty, piano	Columbia L 1494-1496 Columbia (USA) M 25

Le nozze di Figaro, overture

Manchester 29 October 1924	Hallé	Columbia (USA) 67083D Not published in UK

Die Zauberflöte, excerpts (In diesen heiligen Hallen; O Isis und Osiris)

London 9 May 1920	Orchestra Allin Sung in English	Columbia L 1384

MODEST MUSSORGSKY (1839-1881)

Khovantschina, prelude

London 4 March 1924	Orchestra	Columbia L 1573 Columbia (USA) 67053D <u>Abridged version</u>
Manchester 24 June 1929	Hallé	Columbia 9908 Columbia (USA) 67743D Columbia (Japan) J 7614

JACQUES OFFENBACH (1819-1880)

Barcarolle from Les contes d'Hoffmann, arranged for cello and piano

Date not confirmed	Squire Harty, piano	Columbia E 148
Date not confirmed	Squire Harty, piano	Columbia D 1325

HUBERT PARRY (1848-1918)

Blest pair of sirens

Leeds 1927	Leeds Orchestra Leeds, Huddersfield and Sheffield Choirs Coward	Columbia 9222 <u>Recording was not published</u>

GABRIEL PIERNE (1863-1937)

Sérénade, song arranged for cello and piano

London 1916	Squire Harty, piano	Columbia L 1100
Date not confirmed	Sharpe Harty, piano	Columbia E 146

DAVID POPPER (1843-1913)

Alsatian melody for cello and piano

London 1916	Squire Harty, piano	Columbia L 1028

Gavotte no 2 for cello and piano

London 1916	Squire Harty, piano	Columbia L 1028

Papillon for cello and piano

Date not confirmed	Squire Harty, piano	Columbia D 1415

GIACOMO PUCCINI (1858-1924)

La Bohème, excerpt (Che gelida manina)

London 23 September 1919	LSO Burke	Columbia 7205
London 20 July 1923	Orchestra Hackett	Columbia 7273 <u>2 differing takes were made, but the recording was not published</u>
London 13 March 1924	Orchestra Hackett	Columbia 7366
London 15 February 1926	Orchestra Martin	Columbia L 1789

La Bohème, excerpt (Si mi chiamano Mimì)

| London
12 January
1925 | Orchestra
Licette
<u>Sung in English</u> | Columbia L 1665 |

La Bohème, excerpt (Ah Mimì tu più non torni!)

| London
15 February
1926 | Orchestra
Rodrigo, Martin | Columbia L 1763 |

Madama Butterfly, excerpt (Un bel dì)

| London
24 October
1924 | Orchestra
Licette
<u>Sung in English</u> | Columbia L 1666 |

44   Harty

Madama Butterfly, excerpt (Viene la sera)

London 23 May 1920	Orchestra Stralia, Mullings <u>Sung in English</u>	Columbia 7251
London 24 October 1924	Orchestra Licette, Mullings <u>Sung in English</u>	Columbia L 1666

Tosca, excerpt (Vissi d'arte)

London   Orchestra   Columbia L 1706
25 September   Licette
1924

Tosca, excerpt (Tre sbirri, una carrozza)

London   Orchestra   Columbia L 1579
24 June   Formichi   Columbia (USA) 7078M
1924

Tosca, excerpt (Flla verrà per amor del suo Mario!)

London   Orchestra   Columbia L 1949
5 September   Formichi   Columbia (Italy) GQX 16522
1927   Columbia (USA) 7156M
                                         Columbia (Australia) 04061

HENRY PURCELL (1659-1695)

Nymphs and shepherds, chorus from incidental music to The Libertine

Manchester	Hallé	Columbia 9909
24 June	Manchester	45: Columbia SEG 7705/SCD 2092
1929	Childrens Choir	LP: EMI MRS 5141/1C 047 05161M
		CD: ASV CDAJA 5112
		CD: Beulah 2PD 4

JEAN-PHILIPPE RAMEAU (1683-1764)

Menuet from Platée, arranged for cello and piano by Squire

London	Squire	Columbia L 1039
1916	Harty, piano	

MAURICE RAVEL (1875-1937)

Ma mère l'oye, excerpts (Laideronette impératrice des pagodes;Jardin féerique)

Manchester	Hallé	Columbia L 1418
20 October		
1921		

EDWARD EVERETT RICE (1849-1924)

Dear old pal of mine

London	LSO	Columbia 7233
20 January	Burke	
1920		

WILLEM MENGELBERG
and His Concertgebouw Orchestra
(Recorded in the Amsterdam Concert Hall)

Light Blue Label—12-inch, 6/6 each

L1972 { ANACREON—Overture (*Cherubini*)
          Parts 1 and 2
L1973 {   Part 3
          SYMPHONY No. 8—Allegretto scherzando (*Beethoven—Op.* 93)

LIKE a number of operas by other composers, Cherubini's opera, "Anacreon," has passed into the limbo of forgotten things, the only part remaining being the lively and high-spirited overture, and this, with its impeccable craftsmanship, will live for many a long day. It offers many delights to the ear, and with the lovely velvety quality of tone that seems an especial property of the Concertgebouw Orchestra and the realism of the concert hall performance, it will charm in every passage from the delightful wood-wind in the Introduction to the rich string tone in the energetic Allegro movement. The great conductor has given us a record of perfect finish, and the recording reveals every beauty.

Sir HAMILTON HARTY Conducting the
HALLÉ ORCHESTRA
(Recorded in the Free Trade Hall, Manchester)

Light Blue Label—12-inch, 6/6

L1998.—ROSAMUNDE—Overture. In Two Parts (*Schubert*)

WITH his performances of "The Solemn Melody," "Trumpet Voluntary" and "Queen Mab" Scherzo, Sir Hamilton Harty created a new standard in orchestral recording, and now we have an equally glowing rendering of Schubert's lovely "Rosamunde" Overture to match that wonderful trio. Directly the splendidly sonorous great chords of the Andante are heard, it is apparent that here is the finest reproduction this much-loved overture has been given. It only remains to hear it.

WILLIAM MURDOCH—Pianoforte

Light Blue Label—12-inch, 6/6

L1952 { BALLADE in A flat. In Two Parts (*Chopin, Op.* 41)
        (Recorded in the Wigmore Hall, London)

WHAT was the story in Chopin's mind when he wrote this magnificent Ballade? No one really knows, but it calls to mind irresistibly some tale of chivalry and romance, and, as played by Mr. Murdoch here, the music speaks as plainly as words. The rendering is picturesque to a degree and the piano tone is perfect. It gains considerably from the recording in the Wigmore Hall, which has long proved itself ideally suited for the reproduction of chamber music.

Only the NUMBER is necessary when ordering COLUMBIA Records.

"Columbia" NEW PROCESS Records

COLUMBIA MASTERWORKS ALBUM

MOZART
Concertante Sinfonie
for Violin and Viola
(K364)
FOUR RECORDS

Albert Sammons (Violin) and Lionel Tertis (Viola); with the London Philharmonic Orchestra conducted by Sir Hamilton Harty

Columbia

Presented with the Columbia Masterworks Album (No. 148) of the Mozart Concertante Sinfonie.

NIKOLAI RIMSKY-KORSAKOV (1844-1908)

Capriccio espagnol

Manchester 11 February 1929	Hallé	Columbia 9716-9717 Columbia (Japan) J 7516-7517

Flight of the bumble bee (Tsar Sultan)

London 1924	Orchestra	Columbia 980 Columbia (USA) 67096D
Manchester 24 June 1929	Hallé	Columbia 9908 Columbia (USA) 67743D

Introduction and Wedding march (Le coq d'or)

Manchester 24 October 1923	Hallé	Columbia L 1533 Columbia (USA) 67054D

GIOACHINO ROSSINI (1792-1868)

Il barbiere di Siviglia, overture abridged

| Manchester 20 April 1922 | Hallé | Columbia L 1428 |

Semiramide, excerpt (Bel raggio lusinghier)

| London 8 January 1925 | Orchestra Stralia | Columbia 7368 |

La danza, arranged for cello and piano

| Date not confirmed | Squire Harty, piano | Columbia 7895/E 148 |
| Date not confirmed | Squire Harty, piano | Columbia D 1440 |

ANTON RUBINSTEIN (1829-1894)

Melody in F, arranged for cello and piano

| London 1915 | Squire Harty, piano | Columbia L 1003 |
| London 29 August 1922 | Squire Harty, piano | Columbia L 1003 Second version |

CAMILLE SAINT-SAENS (1835-1921)

Cello Concerto No 1

Manchester	Hallé	Columbia L 1800-1802
25 March	Squire	Columbia (USA) M 44
1926		Columbia (Japan) 32

Introduction and Rondo capriccioso for violin and orchestra

London	Orchestra	Columbia L 1335
1919	D.Kennedy	

Le carnaval des animaux

Manchester	Hallé	Columbia L 1617-1619
9 January	Unnamed pianists	Columbia (USA) M 17
1925		

Le cygne (Le carnaval des animaux)

London	Squire	Columbia L 1007
1915	Harty, piano	2 differing takes used
Date not confirmed	Squire Harty, piano	Details not confirmed

Samson et Dalila, excerpt (Maudite à jamais!)

London	Orchestra	Columbia D 1491
1 September	Formichi	Columbia (USA) 2030M
1927		

GIUSEPPE SAMMARTINI (1695-1750)

Old Italian love song, arranged for cello and piano

London 31 August 1922	Squire Harty, piano	Columbia L 1513 <u>This recording was not published</u>
London 12 March 1923	Squire Harty, piano	Columbia L 1513 <u>Second version</u>
London 1 February 1924	Squire Harty, piano	Columbia L 1513 <u>Third version</u>

FRANZ SCHUBERT (1797-1828)

Symphony No 9 "Great"

Manchester 14 January 1928	Hallé	Columbia L 2079-2085 Columbia (USA) M 88

Rosamunde, overture

Manchester 2 May 1927	Hallé	Columbia L 1998 Columbia (USA) 67388D Columbia (Japan) J 1195 LP: Columbia (USA) RL 3033 RL 3033 was not published
Manchester 27 April 1928	Hallé	Columbia L 2122 Columbia (USA) M 343 Columbia (Japan) J 7339/53

Rosamunde, entr'acte no 1

Manchester 27 April 1928	Hallé	Columbia L 2123 Columbia (USA) M 343

Rosamunde, entr'acte no 2

Manchester 27 April 1928	Hallé	Columbia L 2124 Columbia (USA) M 343/M 366

Rosamunde, entr'acte no 3

Manchester 27 April 1928	Hallé	Columbia L 2124 Columbia (USA) M 343

Rosamunde, Shepherds' melody

Manchester 27 April 1928	Hallé	Columbia L 2124 Columbia (USA) M 343

Rosamunde, Ballet music no 1

Manchester 27 April 1928	Hallé	Columbia L 2125 Columbia (USA) M 343

Rosamunde, Ballet music no 2

Manchester 27 April 1928	Hallé	Columbia L 2125 Columbia (USA) M 343

Sonata in A "Arpeggione", arranged by Cassado

London 5 May 1929	Orchestra Cassado	Columbia LX 1-3 Columbia (USA) M 139 Columbia (Japan) 32

Marche militaire, arranged by Guiraud

London 17 November 1933	LPO	Columbia DX 571 Columbia (France) DFX 182 Columbia (USA) 7322M CD: Dutton CDLX 7016

An Sylvia

London 24 July 1923	Orchestra Hackett Sung in English	Columbia 7274 This recording was not published

Wiegenlied, arranged for cello and piano by Squire

Date not confirmed	Squire Harty, piano	Columbia D 1440

54 Harty

ROBERT SCHUMANN (1810-1856)

Violin Sonata in A minor, abridged version of first and second movements

London	D.Kennedy	Columbia L 1338-1339
1919	Harty, piano	

Träumerei, arranged for cello and piano

Date not	Squire	Columbia D 1337
confirmed	Harty, piano	

SELIGMANN

Chanson grècque for cello and piano

Date not	Squire	Columbia D 1434
confirmed	Harty, piano	

JEAN-BAPTISTE SENAILLE (1687-1730)

Allegro spiritoso (Premier livre de sonates), arranged for oboe and orchestra by Camden

London	Orchestra	Columbia L 1826
30 March	Camden	Columbia (USA) M 71
1926		CD: Beulah 1PD 4

The merry harvester, arranged for cello and piano by Squire

Date not	Squire	Columbia D 1372
confirmed	Harty, piano	

JEAN SIBELIUS (1865-1957)

Valse triste

London 17 November 1933	LPO	Columbia DX 571 Columbia (France) DFX 182 Columbia (USA) 7322M CD: Dutton CDLX 7016

LAO SILESU (1883-1953)

Mon coeur est pour toi, arranged for cello and piano by Squire

Date not confirmed	Squire Harty, piano	Columbia D 1369

WILLIAM SQUIRE (1871-1963)

Chansonette

Date not confirmed	Squire Harty, piano	Columbia D 1401

Danse magyare

Date not confirmed	Squire Harty, piano	Columbia D 1425

Danse rustique

Date not confirmed	Squire Harty, piano	Columbia D 1372

Harlequinade

Date not confirmed	Squire Harty, piano	Columbia D 1354

Meditation

London 12 February 1923	Squire Harty, piano	Columbia L 1513

Serenade

London	Squire	Columbia L 1039
1916	Harty, piano	

Tarantella

Date not	Squire	Columbia D 1401
confirmed	Harty, piano	

When you come home

Date not	Squire	Columbia D 1327
confirmed	Harty, piano	

BEDRICH SMETANA (1824-1884)

The Bartered Bride, overture

London 17 November 1933	LPO	Columbia DX 562 Columbia (USA) 7314M CD: Dutton CDLX 7016

CHARLES VILLIERS STANFORD (1852-1924)

Shamus O'Brien, overture

Manchester 20 April 1922	Hallé	Columbia L 1428

RICHARD STRAUSS (1864-1949)

Der Bürger als Edelmann, suite

Manchester 22 October 1923	Hallé	Columbia L 1552 and L 1555-1556 Columbia (USA) M 16

GIUSEPPE TARTINI (1692-1770)

Adagio cantabile for piano trio

London 1910	Renard Trio, of which Harty was probably the pianist	Details not confirmed

PIOTR TCHAIKOVSKY (1840-1893)

Piano Concerto No 1

Manchester 30 November 1929- 8 February 1930	Hallé Solomon	Columbia LX 19-22 Columbia (USA) M 141 Columbia (Japan) 104 CD: Pearl GEMMCD 9478 M 141 uses a different take for side 6

Cossack dance (Mazeppa)

Manchester 12 February 1932	Hallé	Columbia LX 240 Columbia (USA) 9076M

JOHN ROGERS THOMAS

Eileen Alanna

Date not confirmed	Orchestra Butt	Details not confirmed

FRANCIS THOME (1850-1909)

Andante religioso

London 1911	Renard Trio, of which Harty was probably the pianist	Details not confirmed

60 Harty

TUCKER

Genevieve

London 23 March 1921	Orchestra Butt	Columbia 7254

AUGUST VAN BIENE (1850-1913)

The broken melody

London 1915	Squire Harty, piano	Columbia L 1017
London 29 August 1922	Squire Harty, piano	Columbia L 1017 <u>Second version</u>
Date not confirmed	Sharpe Harty, piano	Columbia D 436

Valse apache

Date not confirmed	Squire Harty, piano	Details not confirmed

GIUSEPPE VERDI (1813-1901)

Aida, excerpt (Celeste Aida)

London 14 October 1924	Orchestra Mullings	Columbia L 1349 <u>Previous recording of this aria with same catalogue number but not conducted by Harty</u>
London 25 June 1926	Orchestra O'Sullivan	Columbia L 1816 <u>Later recording of this aria with same catalogue number but not conducted by Harty</u>

Aida, excerpt (Pur ti riveggo)

London 3 May 1920	Orchestra Stralia Mullings <u>Sung in English</u>	Columbia 7248-7249

Ernani, excerpt (Ernani involami!)

London 1915	Orchestra Stralia	Columbia 74005
London 1 January 1925	Orchestra Stralia	Columbia 7329 <u>Previous recording of this aria with same catalogue number but not conducted by Harty</u>

La forza del destino, excerpt (Solenne in quest' ora)

London 15 February 1926	Orchestra Rodrigo, Martin	Columbia L 1763

Otello, excerpt (Credo)

London 2 September 1927	Orchestra Formichi	Columbia L 1949 Columbia (Italy) GQX 1652 Columbia (Australia) 04061

Otello, excerpt (Era la notte)

London 15 October 1924	Orchestra Mullings, H.Williams <u>Sung in English</u>	Columbia L 1604

Otello, excerpt (Ave Maria)

London 12 January 1925	Orchestra Licette <u>Sung in English</u>	Columbia L 1683

Otello, excerpt (Ora e per sempre iddio)

London 18 June 1926	Orchestra Lindi	Columbia L 1773 <u>Later recording of this aria with same catalogue number but not conducted by Harty</u>
London 25-26 June 1926	Orchestra O'Sullivan	Columbia L 1806

Rigoletto, excerpt (Pari siamo)

London 5 September 1927	Orchestra Formichi	Columbia L 2065

Rigoletto, excerpt (Cortigiani!)

London 30 June 1924	Orchestra Formichi	Columbia L 1578

Il trovatore, excerpt (Tacea la notte)

London 8 January 1925	Orchestra Stralia	Columbia 7329 <u>Previous recording of this aria with same catalogue number but not conducted by Harty</u>

Il trovatore, excerpt (Ah si ben mio!)

London 24 June 1920	Orchestra Lindi	Columbia L 1816 <u>Later recording of this aria with same catalogue number but not conducted by Harty</u>

RICHARD WAGNER (1813-1883)

Götterdämmerung, Siegfried's Funeral music

Manchester 24 October 1923	Hallé	Columbia L 1522

Lohengrin, excerpt (Mein Herr und Gott...to end of Act 1)

London 2 December 1925	Orchestra and Chorus Licette, Brunskill, Mullings, Lark, Bate <u>Sung in English</u>	Columbia L 1714/9342

Die Meistersinger von Nürnberg, overture

London 1924	Orchestra	Columbia 976 <u>Some Columbia catalogues incorrectly named conductor as Ketelby</u>

Die Meistersinger von Nürnberg, excerpts (Am stillen Herd; Fanget an!)

London 11 April 1924	Orchestra Mullings <u>Sung in English</u>	Columbia L 1576

Die Meistersinger von Nürnberg, excerpt (Wie duftet doch der Flieder; Wahn, Wahn, überall Wahn!)

London 11 April 1924	Orchestra Allin <u>Sung in English</u>	Columbia L 1591

Parsifal, Karfeitagszauber

London 29 February 1924	Orchestra	Columbia L 1550-1551 Columbia (USA) 67015-67016D

Parsifal, excerpts (Titurel der fromme Held; Du konntest morden?)

London 14 January 1925	Orchestra Allin Sung in English	Columbia L 1628

Siegfried, excerpt (Schmiede, mein Hammer!)

London 8 August 1920	Orchestra Mullings Sung in English	Columbia L 1399 Harty conducts only on the second side of this record; previous recording of the entire extract with same catalogue number but not conducted by Harty

Tannhäuser, excerpt (Dich teure Halle!)

London 5 May 1920	Orchestra Stralia Sung in English	Columbia 7243/7368
London 31 December 1924	Orchestra Stralia	Columbia 7368 Second version

Tannhäuser, excerpt (Allmächtige Jungfrau)

London 14 January 1925	Orchestra Licette	Columbia L 1706

Tannhäuser, excerpt (O Fürstin!)

London 1 May 1920	Orchestra Stralia, Mullings Sung in English	Columbia 7257/7333
London 1 May 1925	Orchestra Stralia, Mullings Sung in English	Columbia 7333 Second version

Tannhäuser, excerpt (Inbrunst im Herzen)

London 5 May 1920	Orchestra Mullings Sung in English	Columbia L 1383
London 30-31 December 1923	Orchestra Mullings Sung in English	Columbia L 1383 Second version A third recording of the extract by Mullings with same catalogue number but not conducted by Harty and not actually published

Tannhäuser, Lied an den Abendstern arrangement for cello and piano

Date not confirmed	Squire Harty, piano	Columbia D 1415

Tristan und Isolde, Tristan's vision

London 29 February 1924	Orchestra	Columbia L 1551 Columbia (USA) 67016D

Die Walküre, excerpt (Leb wohl, du kühnes herrliches Kind!)

London 23 May 1920	Orchestra Allin Sung in English	Columbia L 1390

HENRY WALFORD DAVIES (1869-1941)

Solemn melody

Manchester 2 May 1927	Hallé Dawber, Twelvetrees	Columbia L 1986 Columbia (USA) 7136M Columbia (Japan) J 7189 LP: EMI MRS 5185/1C 047 01632M

WILLIAM WALTON (1902-1983)

Symphony No 1

London 10-11 December 1935	LSO	Decca X 108-113/AX 108-113 Decca (USA) 25600-25605 LP: Decca 414 6591 CD: Dutton CDAX 8003 <u>Premiere recording of the work</u>

CARL MARIA VON WEBER (1786-1826)

Abu Hassan, overture

Manchester 30 April 1927	Hallé	Columbia L 2091 Columbia (USA) M 76/X 34 LP: BBC Records REH 756 Cassette: In Sync C 4130 CD: BBC Records BBCCD 756

Oberon, excerpt (Ozean du Ungeheuer!)

London 23 March 1921	Orchestra Stralia	Columbia 7259
London 1 January 1925	Orchestra Stralia	Columbia 7328 <u>Previous recording of the aria with</u> <u>same catalogue number but not</u> <u>conducted by Harty</u>

JAROMIR WEINBERGER (1896-1967)

Polka and Fugue (Schwanda the Bagpiper)

| Date not confirmed | LSO | Columbia LX 193
Columbia (USA) 68311D |

WILLOUGHBY WEISS (19th century)

The village blacksmith

| London
1920 | Orchestra
Allin | Columbia 787 |

CHARLES WIDOR (1844-1937)

Serenade

| London
1911 | Renard Trio,
of which Harty
was probably
the pianist | Details not confirmed |

WILLIAM WOLSTENHOLME (1865-1931)

Peasant dance for cello and piano

| Date not confirmed | Squire
Harty, piano | Columbia D 1391 |

AMY WOODFORDE-FINDEN (1860-1919)

Kashmiri Love song; Till I wake (4 Indian Love lyrics)

London	Orchestra	Columbia 7245
16 September	Butt	
1920		

<u>A previous recording of the songs by the same artists may exist</u>

HAYDN WOOD (1882-1959)

Wonderful world of romance

London	LSO	Columbia 7240
18 September	Stralia	
1919		

WORMSER

L'enfant prodigue, incidental music

London	Orchestra	Columbia 607-609
1916	Harty, piano	<u>Side 6 of this set may have contained a piano solo by Harty</u>

ALEXANDER ZARZYCKI (1834-1895)

Mazurka for violin and piano

London	D. Kennedy	Columbia L 1339
1919	Harty, piano	

TRADITIONAL AND MISCELLANEOUS

Barbara Allen

Date not confirmed	Orchestra Butt	Columbia X 262

Drink to me only, arranged for cello and piano by Squire

London 1915	Squire Harty, piano	Columbia L 1017 Columbia (USA) A 5832/7068M
London 29 August 1922	Squire Harty, piano	Columbia L 1017 <u>Second version</u>

The First Nowell

Date not confirmed	Orchestra Butt	Columbia X 263/X 307

Londonderry Air, arranged by Harty

London 4 March 1924	Orchestra	Columbia L 1573
Manchester 24 June 1929	Hallé	Columbia 9891 Columbia (Japan) J 7556 LP: BBC Records REH 756 CD: BBC Records BBCCD 756

Mary of Argyle, arranged for cello and piano by Squire

Date not confirmed	Squire Harty, piano	Columbia D 1329

Charles Mackerras
born 1925

with valuable assistance from Malcolm Walker

Discography compiled by John Hunt

CHARLES MACKERRAS

PHILHARMONIA ORCHESTRA

★

SULLIVAN

"IOLANTHE" OVERTURE
"RUDDIGORE" OVERTURE

"HIS MASTER'S VOICE"
EXTENDED PLAY 45 R.P.M. RECORD

Photo: Derek Allen

TOMASO ALBINONI (1671-1751)

Concerti in B flat and D

London 23-25 January 1977	English Chamber Orchestra André	LP: EMI ASD 3394/1C 065 02896/ 　　2C 069 02896/EG 29 04941 CD: EMI CDM 763 5282/CMS 769 8802

ALBERT ARLEN (Born 1905)

Clancy of the Overflow

London 4 May 1955	LSO Dawson	45: HMV 7EG 8157 LP: HMV (Australia) SM 411-414 LP: World Records (Australia) PD 1

THOMAS ARNE (1710-1778)

Where the bee sucks

London 26-27 April 1964	Pro Arte Orchestra Harwood	LP: EMI CLP 1789/CSD 1542/ESD 7002/ 　　MFP 1014

JUAN CRISOSTOMO ARRIAGA (1806-1826)

Symphony in D

Glasgow   Scottish CO   CD: Hyperion CDA 66800
1995

Los esclavos felices, overture

Glasgow   Scottish CO   CD: Hyperion CDA 66800
1995

DANIEL FRANCOIS AUBER (1782-1871)

Les rendez-vous

London   Sadlers Wells   Columbia unpublished
11 July   Orchestra
1951

CARL PHILIPP EMANUEL BACH (1714-1788)

Flute Concerto in D minor

| London 1978 | English Chamber Orchestra Dingfelder | LP: Enigma ACM 2020 LP: Nonesuch H 71388 CD: ASV CDQS 6012 |

JOHANN SEBASTIAN BACH (1685-1750)

Ave Maria, arranged by Gounod

| London 25 May- 1 July 1957 | Philharmonia Orchestra & Chorus Schwarzkopf | Columbia unpublished |

The Wise Virgins, ballet suite arranged by Walton

| London 28 March 1982 | English Chamber Orchestra | CD: Radio Classics 15656 91612 |

BELA BARTOK (1881-1945)

Rumanian Folk Dances, arranged by Szekely

London 31 October 1960	Philharmonia	LP: Columbia 33SX 1389/SCX 3427 LP: Capitol P 8660/SP 8660

ARNOLD BAX (1883-1953)

Coronation march

London 12-14 August 1975	LPO	LP: Readers' Digest RDS 8024

LUDWIG VAN BEETHOVEN (1770-1827)

Symphony No 1

Manchester　　　　Royal Liverpool PO　CD: EMI CDEMX 2246/CDM 565 7892
9-10
September
1994

Symphony No 3 "Eroica"

Manchester　　　　Royal Liverpool PO　CD: EMI CDEMX 2246/CDM 565 7892
9-10
September
1994

Symphony No 4

Manchester　　　　Royal Liverpool PO　CD: EMI CDEMX 2245/CDM 565 7882
26 November
1994

Symphony No 5

Liverpool　　　　　Royal Liverpool PO　CD: EMI CDEMX 2212/CDM 764 8012
25-26
June
1992

Symphony No 6 "Pastoral"

Manchester　　　　Royal Liverpool PO　CD: EMI CDEMX 2245/CDM 565 7882
26 November
1994

Symphony No 7

Liverpool 25-26 June 1992	Royal Liverpool PO	CD: EMI CDEMX 2212/CDM 764 8012

Symphony No 9 "Choral"

Liverpool January 1991	Royal Liverpool PO and Chorus Rodgers, D.Jones, Bronder, Terfel	CD: EMI CDEMX 2186/CDM 764 1762

Piano Concerto No 2, arranged by Cooper

Petersham 26-29 November 1993	English Chamber Orchestra Kazakevich	CD: Conifer CDCF 237

Piano Concerto No 4 arranged by Cooper

Petersham 26-29 November 1993	English Chamber Orchestra Kazakevich	CD: Conifer CDCF 237

Violin Concerto

London 24-25 November 1992	Orchestra of Age of Enlightenment Huggett	CD: EMI CDEMX 2217/CDM 565 0272

Die Geschöpfe des Prometheus, incidental music

Glasgow   Scottish CO   CD: Hyperion CDA 66748
18-19
April
1994

Turkish March (Die Ruinen von Athen)

London   LPO   LP: Readers' Digest RDS 8024
12-14
August
1975

ALBAN BERG (1835-1935)

7 frühe Lieder

London   New Philharmonia   EMI unpublished
7 May   C.Ludwig   <u>Recording incomplete</u>
1968

HECTOR BERLIOZ (1803-1869)

Le carnaval romain, overture

London 27 October 1956	Philharmonia	LP: HMV DLP 1177 LP: Angel 35750

La damnation de Faust, Ballet des sylphes

London 23-24 October 1956	Philharmonia	45: HMV 7EP 7112/PES 5269 LP: HMV DLP 1168 LP: Angel 35750

La damnation de Faust, Marche hongroise

London 23-24 October 1956	Philharmonia	45: HMV 7EP 7112/PES 5269 LP: HMV DLP 1168 LP: Angel 35750
London 12-14 August 1975	LPO	LP: Readers' Digest RDS 8024

La damnation de Faust, Menuet des follets

London 23-24 October 1956	Philharmonia	45: HMV 7EP 7112/PES 5269 LP: HMV DLP 1168 LP: Angel 35750

Le jeune pâtre breton

London 9 January 1979	Philharmonia J.Smith	CD: Radio Classics 15656 91532

Les nuits d'été

London 9 January 1979	Philharmonia J.Smith	CD: Radio Classics 15656 91532

Les troyens, Marche troyenne

London 23-24 October 1956	Philharmonia	LP: HMV DLP 1168 LP: Angel 35750

RONALD BINGE (1910-1979)

The Grand Old Duke of York ; The Story of Cock Robin

| London
11-12
January
1962 | Pro Arte
Orchestra
Brannigan | LP: HMV CLP 1557/CSD 1437 |

ERNEST BLOCH (1880-1959)

Schelomo for cello and orchestra

| Watford
19 February
1990 | LPO
Harnoy | CD: RCA/BMG RD 60757 |

ALEXANDER BORODIN (1833-1887)

Prince Igor, overture and Polovtsian dances

Liverpool Date not confirmed	Royal Liverpool PO	CD: Virgin CUV 561 1352/VC 759 6252

WILLIAM BOYCE (1711-1779)

Hearts of oak, arranged by Tomlinson

London 26-27 April 1964	Pro Arte Orchestra Brannigan	LP: EMI CLP 1789/CSD 1542/ ESD 7002/MFP 1014

JOHANNES BRAHMS (1833-1897)

Symphony No 1

Hamburg 14-18 May 1967	Philharmonisches Staatsorchester	LP: Checkmate (USA) 76001
Edinburgh 6-30 January 1997	Scottish CO	CD: Telarc CD 80450

Symphony No 2

Edinburgh 6-30 January 1997	Scottish CO	CD: Telarc CD 80450

Symphony No 3

Edinburgh 6-30 January 1997	Scottish CO	CD: Telarc CD 80450

Symphony No 4

Edinburgh 6-30 January 1997	Scottish CO	CD: Telarc CD 80450

The Telarc set of Brahms symphonies contains a discussion between Mackerras and Alyn Shipton about these chamber-sized recordings

Violin Concerto

London 21-23 May 1985	LSO Udagawa	CD: Chandos CHAN 8974

Haydn Variations

Edinburgh 6-30 January 1997	Scottish CO	CD: Telarc CD 80450

Hungarian Dance No 1

Walthamstow 23 July 1961	LSO	LP: Philips GL 5698/6747 071 LP: Philips (USA) PHS 900.022 CD: Mercury 434 3522

Hungarian Dance No 5

London 31 October 1960	Philharmonia	45: Columbia SED 5578/ESD 7268 LP: Columbia 33SX 1389/SCX 3427

Hungarian Dance No 6

London 31 October 1960	Philharmonia	45: Columbia SED 5578/ESD 7368 LP: Columbia 33SX 1389/SCX 3427

Hungarian Dance No 20

Walthamstow 23 July 1961	LSO	LP: Philips GL 5698/6747 050 LP: Philips (USA) PHM 500.022/ PHS 900.022

Hungarian Dance No 21

Walthamstow 23 July 1961	LSO	LP: Philips GL 5698/6747 050 LP: Philips (USA) PHM 500.022/ PHS 900.022

Sandmännchen, arranged by Mackerras

London 25 May– 1 July 1957	Philharmonia Orchestra & Chorus Schwarzkopf	LP: Columbia 33CX 1482 LP: Angel 35580/36750 LP: EMI ASD 3798/100 4531 CD: EMI CDM 763 5742

HAVERGAL BRIAN (1876-1972)

Symphony No 7

Liverpool 3-4 May 1987	Royal Liverpool PO	CD: EMI CDM 764 1792

Symphony No 31

Liverpool 3-4 May 1987	Royal Liverpool PO	CD: EMI CDM 764 1792

The Tinker's Wedding, overture

Liverpool 3-4 May 1987	Royal Liverpool PO	CD: EMI CDM 764 1792

BENJAMIN BRITTEN (1913-1976)

Gloriana

Swansea 26 October- 6 November 1992	Welsh National Opera Orchestra and Chorus Barstow, Kenny, D.Jones, Langridge, Summers, Opie, Van Allan, Terfel	CD: Decca 440 2132

Variations and Fugue on a theme of Purcell

London 1994	LSO Kingsley	CD: Cala CACD 1022

MAX BRUCH (1838-1920)

Violin Concerto No 1

London 21-23 May 1985	LSO Udagawa	CD: Chandos CHAN 8974

Kol Nidrei for cello and orchestra

Watford 19 February- London 25 November 1990	LPO Harnoy	CD: RCA/BMG RD 60757

Canzone for cello and orchestra

Watford 19 February- London 25 November 1990	LPO Harnoy	CD: RCA/BMG RD 60757

Adagio on Celtic themes for cello and orchestra

Watford 19 February- London 25 November 1990	LPO Harnoy	CD: RCA/BMG RD 60757

Ave Maria for cello and orchestra

Watford 19 February- London 25 November 1990	LPO Harnoy	CD: RCA/BMG RD 60757

PAUL BURKHARD (1911-1977)

Der Schuss von der Kanzel, overture

London 4 June 1956	RPO	45: HMV 7EP 7037

FERRUCCIO BUSONI (1866-1924)

Comedy Overture

Walthamstow 8 February 1969	LSO	CD: Radio Classics 15656 91372

EMILIO DE CAVALIERI (1550-1602)

Rappresentazione di anima e di corpo

Vienna 17-24 February 1970	Capella academica Vienna Chamber Choir Zylis-Gara, Moser, Geszty, Auger, Troyanos, Equiluz, Esswood, Adam, Prey	LP: DG 2708 016 CD: DG 453 1652

EMMANUEL CHABRIER (1841-1894)

España

London 27 October 1956	Philharmonia	45: HMV 7EP 7109/PES 5268 LP: HMV DLP 1177 LP: Angel 35750

Fête polonaise (Le roi malgré lui)

London 26 October 1956	Philharmonia	45: HMV 7EP 7109/PES 5268 LP: HMV DLP 1177 LP: Angel 35750

Joyeuse marche

London 12-14 April 1975	LPO	LP: Readers' Digest RDS 8024

GUSTAVE CHARPENTIER (1860-1950)

Louise, excerpt (Depuis le jour)

London 22-27 May 1969	RPO Sills	LP: EMI ASD 2513/1C 063 90370/ 2C 069 90370 LP: ABC (USA) WST 17163

ERNEST CHAUSSON (1855-1899)

Poème pour violon et orchestre

London 27 April- 18 May 1969	LSO Zukerman	LP: CBS MS 7422/72828

LUIGI CHERUBINI (1760-1842)

Symphony in D

Walthamstow 8 February 1969	LSO	CD: Radio Classics 15656 91372

FREDERIC CHOPIN (1810-1849)

Les sylphides, ballet arranged by Jacob

London 25 May 1959	Philharmonia	LP: Columbia 33SX 1207/SCX 3291 LP: Angel 35833 LP: EMI MFP 2075 <u>Excerpts</u> 45: Columbia SED 5570/SED 5571/ ESD 7262/ESD 7263

JEREMIAH CLARKE (1674-1707)

Trumpet Voluntary

London 4 April 1956	LSO brass Eskdale	45: HMV 7EP 7031/7P 269

ERIC COATES (1886-1957)

At the dance (Summer Days suite)

London 23-24 May 1956	LSO	45: Columbia SED 5539 LP: Columbia 33S 1092 LP: EMI XLP 30071/CFP 40279 CD: EMI CFPD 41 44563

By the sleepy lagoon

London 23-24 May 1956	LSO	78: Columbia DB 8966 45: Columbia SED 5539/SCD 2190 LP: Columbia 33S 1092 LP: EMI XLP 30071/CFP 40279 CD: EMI CFPD 41 44563

Man from the sea (Three Men suite)

London 23-24 May 1956	LSO	LP: Columbia 33S 1092 LP: EMI XLP 30071/CFP 40279 CD: EMI CFPD 41 44563

The Merrymakers, overture

London	LSO	45: Columbia SED 5539
23-24		LP: Columbia 33S 1092
May		LP: EMI XLP 30071/CFP 40279
1956		CD: EMI CFPD 41 44563

Oxford Street march (London Suite Again)

London	LSO	45: Columbia SED 5539/SCD 2190
23-24		LP: Columbia 33S 1092
May		LP: EMI XLP 30071/CFP 40279
1956		

Queen Elizabeth march (The 3 Elizabeths suite)

London	LSO	LP: Columbia 33S 1092
23-24		LP: EMI XLP 30071/CFP 40279
May		
1956		

The 3 Bears fantasy

London	LSO	LP: Columbia 33S 1092
23-24		LP: EMI XLP 30071/CFP 40279
May		CD: EMI CFPD 41 44563
1956		

AARON COPLAND (1900-1990)

The Quiet City

London	Philharmonia	HMV unpublished
30 April-		
November		
1956		

Hoe Down (Rodeo)

London	Philharmonia	HMV unpublished
25 April		
1956		

El salón México

London	Philharmonia	HMV unpublished
23-24		
October		
1956		

CLAUDE DEBUSSY (1862-1918)

La mer

London	LSO	LP: Centaur CRC 1007
August		
1980		

LEO DELIBES (1836-1891)

Coppélia, ballet suite

London 1-2 April 1969	New Philharmonia	LP: EMI TWO 275/CFP 40229 LP: Angel 60284

Lakmé, ballet music

London 16 April 1956	Covent Garden Orchestra	45: HMV 7EP 7069

La source, ballet music

London 23 April 1956	Covent Garden Orchestra	LP: HMV CLP 1195 LP: EMI XLP 30022/SXLP 30022/CFP 40298

Sylvia, ballet suite

London 8-9 May 1968	New Philharmonia	LP: EMI TWO 275/CFP 40229 LP: Angel 60284

SADLER'S WELLS

Re-opened by LILIAN BAYLIS, January 6th, 1931

OPERA
AND
BALLET

1951-52 SEASON

WEDNESDAY EVENING, JUNE 6th, 1951

KATYA KABANOVA

(LEOS JANACEK)

Opera in Three Acts (after Ostrovsky's "The Storm.")
(By arrangement with Alfred A. Kalmus (Universal Edition), London.)
English translation by Norman Tucker.

Conductor : CHARLES MACKERRAS

Producer : DENNIS ARUNDELL
Settings devised by DENNIS ARUNDELL and JOHN GLASS
Designs by JOHN GLASS and L. W. ANSON
Costumes by ANTHONY BOYES

Characters in order of singing

Vanya, *clerk to Dikoy* .. .. ROBERT THOMAS
Glasha, *servant in the Kabanov household* SHEILA REX
Dikoy, *a rich merchant* .. STANLEY CLARKSON
Boris Grigorievitch, *his nephew* .. ROWLAND JONES
Feklusha, *servant in the Kabanov household*
ROSE CARLTON
Marfa Kabanova (Kabanicha), *a rich merchant's widow*
KATE JACKSON
Tichon Kabanov, *her son* .. JOHN KENTISH
Barbara, *fosterchild in the Kabanov household*
MARION STUDHOLME
Katerina Kabanova (Katya), *Tichon's wife*
AMY SHUARD
Kuligin, *friend of Vanya* HAROLD BLACKBURN

A woman in the crowd, a passer-by, townspeople

FREDERICK DELIUS (1862-1934)

A Village Romeo and Juliet

Vienna 1-13 January 1989	Austrian RO Schoenberg Choir Field, Davies, Dean, Hampson	CD: Decca 430 2752 VHS Video: Decca 071 1343 Laserdisc: Decca 071 1341 Video version uses soundtrack only as basis of a film version with actors

A Village Romeo and Juliet, prelude

Swansea 20 December 1990	Welsh National Opera Orchestra	CD: Decca 430 2022

Cello Concerto

Liverpool July 1991	Royal Liverpool PO Wallfisch	CD: EMI CDEMX 2185/CDM 764 1752

Violin Concerto

Swansea 11-12 May 1991	Welsh National Opera Orchestra Little	CD: Decca 433 7042

Double Concerto

Liverpool July 1991	Royal Liverpool PO Little, Wallfisch	CD: EMI CDEMX 2185/CDM 764 1752

Appalachia

Swansea April 1993	Welsh National Opera Orchestra and Chorus Washington	CD: Decca 443 1712

Aquarelles

Swansea 11-12 May 1991	Welsh National Opera Orchestra	CD: Decca 433 7042

Brigg Fair

Swansea August 1989	Welsh National Opera Orchestra	CD: Decca 430 2022

2 Dance Rhapsodies

Swansea 11-12 May 1991	Welsh National Opera Orchestra	CD: Decca 433 7042

Fennimore and Gerda, intermezzo

Swansea 20 December 1990	Welsh National Opera Orchestra	CD: Decca 433 7042

Florida suite

Swansea August 1990	Welsh National Opera Orchestra	CD: Decca 430 2062

In a summer garden

Swansea August 1989	Welsh National Opera Orchestra	CD: Decca 430 2022

Irmelin, prelude

Swansea 20 December 1990	Welsh National Opera Orchestra	CD: Decca 433 7042

North Country Sketches

Swansea August 1989	Welsh National Opera Orchestra	CD: Decca 430 2022

On hearing the first cuckoo in spring

Swansea 20 December 1990	Welsh National Opera Orchestra	CD: Decca 433 7042

Over the hills and far away

Swansea April 1993	Welsh National Opera Orchestra	CD: Decca 443 1712

Paris

Liverpool July 1991	Royal Liverpool PO	CD: EMI CDEMX 2185/CDM 764 1752

Sea Drift

Swansea August 1990	Welsh National Opera Orchestra and Chorus Hampson	CD: Decca 430 2062

Song of the high hills

Swansea April 1993	Welsh National Opera Orchestra Evans, Hoare	CD: Decca 443 1712

Summer night on the river

Swansea 20 December 1990	Welsh National Opera Orchestra	CD: Decca 433 7042

ERNO DOHNANYI (1877-1960)

Konzertstück for cello and orchestra

London	LSO	CD: Chandos CHAN 8662
4-5	Wallfisch	
July		
1988		

GAETONO DONIZETTI (1797-1848)

Don Pasquale, overture

Watford 18-24 July 1959	Pro Arte Orchestra	45: Pye CEM 36016/CSEM 75007 LP: Pye GGC 4011/GSGC 14011 LP: Vanguard SRV 178

La fille du régiment, overture

Watford 18-24 July 1959	Pro Arte Orchestra	45: Pye CEM 36016/CSEM 75007 LP: Pye GGC 4011/GSGC 14011 LP: Vanguard SRV 178

Lucia di Lammermoor

Edinburgh August 1997	Hanover Band Edinburgh Festival Chorus Rost, Ford, Davies, Miles, Michaels-Moore	CD: Sony awaiting publication

Maria Stuarda

London 1-22 April 1982	English National Opera Orchestra and Chorus Baker, Plowright, Rendall, Opie, Tomlinson <u>Sung in English</u>	LP: EMI SLS 5277 LP: Angel 3927
London Date not confirmed	English National Opera Orchestra and Chorus Baker, Plowright, Rendall, Opie, Tomlinson <u>Sung in English</u>	VHS Video: Castle CVI 2038

Poliuto, excerpt (Ah fuggi da morte!)

London 31 March- 10 April 1970	LSO Caballé, Marti	LP: EMI ASD 2723

Roberto Devereux

London 1-5 June 1969	RPO Ambrosian Singers Sills, Wolff, Ilosfalvy, MacDonald, Glossop	LP: EMI SLS 787 LP: ABC (USA) ATS 20003/WST 323 LP: Angel 34033 Excerpts LP: ABC (USA) ATS 20008 LP: Angel 34015

PAUL DUKAS (1865-1935)

L'apprenti sorcier

London 1994	LSO	CD: Cala CACD 1022

ANTONIN DVORAK (1841-1904)

Symphony No 7

London 21-23 May 1991	LPO	CD: EMI CDEMX 2202/CDM 764 6582

Symphony No 8

Hamburg 14-18 May 1967	Philharmonisches Staatsorchester	LP: Nonesuch H 71262
London 26-29 April 1992	LPO	CD: EMI CDEMX 2216/CDM 565 0262

Symphony No 9 "From the New World"

London 21-23 May 1991	LPO	CD: EMI CDEMX 2202/CDM 764 6582

Cello Concerto

London 4-5 July 1988	LSO Wallfisch	CD: Chandos CHAN 8662

Romance for violin and orchestra

London 20-21 May 1994	English Chamber Orchestra Gonley	CD: EMI CDEMX 2232/CDM 565 4622

Serenade for strings

London 13-14 February 1983	English Chamber Orchestra	LP: EMI EMX 2013 CD: EMI CDCFP 4597

Symphonic Variations

London 26-29 April 1992	LPO	CD: EMI CDEMX 2216/CDM 565 0262

Czech Suite

Wembley 1 June 1969	English Chamber Orchestra	LP: Philips 6500 203/6527 129/420 2981 CD: Philips 442 6602

10 Legends

London 20-21 May 1994	English Chamber Orchestra	CD: EMI CDEMX 2232/CDM 565 4622

Nocturne for strings

London 20-21 May 1994	English Chamber Orchestra	CD: EMI CDEMX 2232/CDM 565 4622

4 Slavonic Dances: nos 1, 2, 3 and 10

London 28 September- 31 October 1960	Philharmonia	LP: Columbia 33SX 1389/SCX 3427 LP: Capitol P 8660/SP 8660 LP: EMI CFP 40214

EDWARD ELGAR (1857-1934)

Symphony No 1

Walthamstow April 1990	LSO	CD: Decca 430 8352

Symphony No 2

Walthamstow 15-16 April 1993	RPO	CD: Decca 443 3212

Cello Concerto

Walthamstow 24-25 February 1992	RPO Cohen	CD: Decca 436 5452

Romance for cello and orchestra

London 21-22 April 1986	LSO Lloyd-Webber	LP: EMI EL 27 04301 CD: EMI CDC 747 6222/CDM 764 7262

Enigma Variations

London 13 March 1985	LPO	LP: EMI EL 27 03741 CD: EMI CDC 747 4162/CDB 572 1382
Walthamstow 24-25 February 1992	RPO	CD: Decca 436 5452

Starlight Express, incidental music

Swansea December 1990	Welsh National Opera Orchestra Hagley, Terfel	CD: Decca 433 2142

Sea Pictures

Walthamstow 15-16 April 1993	RPO D.Jones	CD: Decca 443 3212

Cockaigne, overture

Walthamstow April 1990	LSO	CD: Decca 430 8352

Dream Children, 2 pieces for small orchestra

Swansea December 1990	Welsh National Opera Orchestra	CD: Decca 433 2142

Falstaff

London 11-12 March 1985	LPO	LP: EMI EL 27 03741 CD: EMI CDC 747 4162

Froissart, overture

Walthamstow 24-25 February 1992	RPO	CD: Decca 436 5452

Imperial march

London 12-14 April 1975	LPO	LP: Readers' Digest RDS 8024

Wand of Youth, suites 1 and 2

Swansea December 1990	Welsh National Opera Orchestra	CD: Decca 433 2142

GEORGES ENESCO (1881-1955)

Rumanian Rhapsody No 1

London 31 October 1960	Philharmonia	LP: Columbia 33SX 1389/SCX 3427

MANUEL DE FALLA (1876-1946)

El sombrero de 3 picos, 3 dances

Walthamstow 18-24 July 1959	Pro Arte Orchestra	45: Pye CEM 36013 LP: Pye GGC 4011/GSGC 14011 LP: Vanguard SRV 178 <u>According to Guide to the Bargain Classics (LP Record Library 1965) this could be a recording by LPO conducted by Rignold</u>

GABRIEL FAURE (1845-1924)

Elégie pour violoncello et orchestre

London 5-7 May 1976	New Philharmonia H.Schiff	LP: DG 2530 793 CD: DG 431 1662

JOHN FIELD (1782-1837)

Piano Concerto No 2

Edinburgh 27 February- 1 March 1993	Scottish Chamber Orchestra O'Conor	CD: Telarc CD 80370

Piano Concerto No 3

Edinburgh 27 February- 1 March 1993	Scottish Chamber Orchestra O'Conor	CD: Telarc CD 80370

CESAR FRANCK (1822-1890)

Panis angelicus, arranged by Mackerras

London 25 May- 1 July 1957	Philharmonia Orchestra & Chorus Schwarzkopf	LP: Columbia 33CX 1482 LP: Angel 35530/36750 LP: EMI ASD 3798/100 5431 CD: EMI CDM 763 5742

UMBERTO GIORDANO (1867-1948)

Andrea Chenier, excerpt (Vicino a te)

London 31 March- 10 April 1970	LSO Caballé, Marti	LP: EMI ASD 2723

ALEXANDER GLAZUNOV (1865-1936)

Concert waltz no 1

London 25 October 1956	Philharmonia	LP: HMV DLP 1170

REINHOLD GLIERE (1875-1956)

Russian Sailors' Dance (The Red Poppy)

London 25 October 1956	Philharmonia	LP: HMV DLP 1170

MIKHAIL GLINKA (1804-1857)

Russlan and Ludmila, overture

London 25 October 1956	Philharmonia	45: HMV 7EP 7084 LP: HMV DLP 1170
Barking 4-15 June 1970	LPO	LP: EMI CFP 101

Jota aragonesa

Walthamstow 22 July 1961	LSO	LP: Philips 6747 050 CD: Mercury 434 3522

CHRISTOPH WILLIBALD GLUCK (1714-1787)

Orfeo ed Euridice, arranged by Mackerras

Vienna	VPO	LP: Vanguard BGS 70686-70687/
19-22	Akademiechor	VSL 11004-11005/HM 66-67
June	Stich-Randall,	CD: Vanguard 08.404072
1966	Steffek, Forrester	<u>Orchestra described for this recording as Vienna State Opera Orchestra</u>

Orfeo ed Euridice, ballet music

Walthamstow	LSO	LP: Mercury WS 9002
19-23		
July		
1961		

FREDERICK GLUCK (19th century)

In einem kühlen Grunde, arranged by Mackerras

London	Philharmonia	LP: Columbia 33CX 1482
25 May-	Orchestra & Chorus	LP: Angel 35530/36750
1 July	Schwarzkopf	LP: EMI ASD 3798/100 5431
1957		CD: EMI CDM 763 5742

CHARLES GOUNOD (1818-1893)

Faust

Cardiff May 1996	Welsh National Opera Orchestra and Chorus Watson, Clarke, Miles <u>Sung in English</u>	Unpublished video recording

Faust, excerpt (Soldiers' chorus)

London 12-14 August 1975	LPO	LP: Readers' Digest RDS 8024

Faust, ballet music

London 22 October 1956	Philharmonia	LP: HMV DLP 1177
London 9 May 1968- 2 April 1969	New Philharmonia	LP: EMI TWO 275/CFP 40229 LP: Angel 60284

EDVARD GRIEG (1843-1907)

2 Elegiac melodies

Walthamstow 27-30 May 1958	LSO	LP: RCA LM 2336/LSC 2336/RB 16179/ SB 2069/VIC 1069/VICS 1069 LP: Decca SPA 91/VIV 44 LP: London STS 15159

Cowkeeper's tune and Country dance (2 Norwegian melodies)

Walthamstow 27-30 May 1958	LSO	LP: RCA LM 2336/LSC 2336/RB 16179/ SB 2069/VIC 1069/VICS 1069 LP: Decca SPA 91/SPA 421 LP: London STS 15159

Wedding Day at Troldhaugen (Lyric Pieces), arranged by Huppertz

Walthamstow 27-30 May 1958	LSO	LP: RCA LM 2336/LSC 2336/RB 16179/ SB 2069/VIC 1069/VICS 1069 LP: Decca SPA 91 LP: London STS 15159

FRANZ XAVER GRUBER (1787-1863)

Stille Nacht, heilige Nacht

London 25 May- 1 July 1957	Philharmonia Orchestra & Chorus Schwarzkopf	LP: Columbia 33CX 1482 LP: Angel 35530/36750 LP: EMI ASD 3798/100 5431 CD: EMI CDM 763 5742

JOHAN HALVORSEN (1864-1935)

Entry of the Boyards

London 12-14 August 1975	LPO	LP: Readers' Digest RDS 8024

GEORGE FRIDERIC HANDEL (1685-1759)

Messiah, arranged by Lam

London
29 June-
9 August
1966
	English Chamber
	Orchestra
	Ambrosian Singers
	Harwood, Baker,
	Esswood, Tear,
	Herincx
		LP: EMI RLS 693/SLS 774/
		    1C 153 00635-00637
		LP: Angel 3705
		CD: EMI CZS 762 7482/CZS 569 4492
		<u>Excerpts</u>
		LP: EMI YKM 5007/SEOM 13/CFP 40277/
		    HQS 1183/HQS 1244/1C 047 28592/
		    1C 053 01881
		LP: Angel 36530
		CD: EMI CDM 565 3362/CMS 565 8512

Messiah, arranged by Mozart

Vienna 31 January- 4 February 1974	Austrian Radio Orchestra & Chorus Mathis, Finnilä, Schreier, Adam	LP: DG 2710 016/2723 019 CD: DG 427 1732

Judas Maccabaeus

Watford 4-12 April 1976	English Chamber Orchestra Wandsworth Choir Palmer, Baker, Esswood, Davies, Shirley-Quirk, Keyte	LP: DG 2710 021/413 9091

Saul

Leeds 18-21 May 1972	English Chamber Orchestra Leeds Festival Chorus M.Price, Armstrong, Davies, Bowman, English, McIntyre, Dean	LP: DG 2722 008/2710 014

Israel in Egypt

Leeds 15-17 April 1970	English Chamber Orchestra Leeds Festival Chorus Harper, P.Clark, Esswood, Young, Rippon, Keyte	LP: DG 2708 020/413 9191 CD: DG 429 5302

Giulio Cesare

London August 1984	English National Opera Orchestra and Chorus Masterson, Baker, S.Walker, D.Jones, Bowman, Tomlinson Sung in English	LP: EMI EX 27 02323 CD: EMI CMS 769 7602
London Date not confirmed	English National Opera Orchestra and Chorus Masterson, Baker, S.Walker, D.Jones, Bowman, Tomlinson Sung in English	VHS Video: Pioneer PLMCD 771 VHS Video: Polygram 079 2463 VHS Video: MCEG VVD 383

Serse

London 1988	English National Opera Orchestra and Chorus Masterson, Garrett, Murray, Rigby, Robson, Booth-Jones Sung in English	VHS Video: Polydor 079 2933

Berenice, overture

London 4 April 1956	LSO	45: HMV 7EP 7031/7P 269

Organ Concerti

London 14-23 August 1963	Pro Arte Orchestra Germani	HMV unpublished <u>Recordings incomplete</u>

Concerti grossi op 3

Prague 18-19 February 1978	Prague Chamber Orchestra	LP: EMI ESD 7089/EMX 41 20861/1C065 03419 LP: Angel 34497

Sonata for trumpet and strings, arranged by Thilde

London
23-25
January
1977
	English Chamber
	Orchestra
	André
		LP: EMI ASD 3394/1C 065 02896/
		   2C 069 02896/EG 29 04941
		CD: EMI CDM 763 5282/CZS 767 8942/
		   CZS 769 8802

Water Music

Prague 1-4 February 1978	Prague Chamber Orchestra	LP: EMI ASD 3597/ED 10 32711/1C065 03271 LP: Angel 37532/34497 <u>Excerpts</u> LP: EMI ESD 143 6131 CD: EMI CDCFP 4613

Water Music, suite arranged by Harty

London 4 April 1956	LSO	45: HMV 7EP 7031
New York 14-15 March 1991	Orchestra of St. Lukes	CD: Telarc CD 80279

Music for the Royal Fireworks, arranged by Mackerras

London 13-14 April 1959	Wind ensemble	LP: Pye CML 33005/ GGC 4003/GSGC 14003/ GSGC 2018/GSGC 15009 LP: Vanguard SRV 289/MST 27 LP: Eurodisc 200 887.315
London 8 October- 19 December 1976	LSO	LP: EMI ASD 3395/ED 10 28941/ ESD 143 6131/1C 065 02894 LP: Angel 37404 <u>This version includes the 3 Concerti</u> <u>a due cori also listed below in</u> <u>separate recordings</u>
London December 1993	English Chamber Orchestra	CD: Nova 150.1022

Concerto a due cori No 1

London December 1993	English Chamber Orchestra	CD: Nova 150.1022

Concerto a due cori No 2

London 13-14 April 1959	Pro Arte Orchestra	LP: Pye CML 33005/ GGC 4003/GSGC 14003/ GSGC 2018/GSGC 15009 LP: Vanguard SRV 289 LP: Eurodisc 200 887.315
London December 1993	English Chamber Orchestra	CD: Nova 150.1022

Concerto a due cori No 3

London December 1993	English Chamber Orchestra	CD: Nova 150.1022

<u>At time of going to press the French label Forlane has announced a CD of</u>
<u>Handel arias, in which Mackerras conducts Ann Murray and the Orchestra of</u>
<u>the Enlightenment</u>

FRANZ JOSEF HAYDN (1732-1809)

Symphony No 18

London 1 February 1969	LSO	LP: Columbia (USA) 3216 0342

Symphony No 31 "Horn Signal"

Engelwood NJ 8-9 November 1988	Orchestra of St Lukes	CD: Telarc CD 80156

Symphony No 45 "Farewell"

Engelwood NJ 8-9 November 1988	Orchestra of St Lukes	CD: Telarc CD 80156

Symphony No 80

Sydney 11-15 August 1983	Australian Chamber Orchestra	LP: CBS (Australia) DBR 005

Symphony No 81

Sydney 11-15 August 1983	Australian Chamber Orchestra	LP: CBS (Australia) DBR 005

Symphony No 100 "Military"

New York 12-14 March 1991	Orchestra of St Lukes	CD: Telarc CD 80282

Symphony No 101 "Clock"

New York 7-9 March 1992	Orchestra of St Lukes	CD: Telarc CD 80311

Symphony No 103 "Drum Roll"

New York 12-14 March 1991	Orchestra of St Lukes	CD: Telarc CD 80282

Symphony No 104 "London"

New York 7-9 March 1992	Orchestra of St Lukes	CD: Telarc CD 80311

MICHAEL HAYDN (1737-1806)

Symphony in D minor

Denham 28-29 December 1970	English Chamber Orchestra	LP: DG 2533 074

Symphony in G, with introduction by Mozart

Denham 28-29 December 1970	English Chamber Orchestra	LP: DG 2533 074

Symphony in D (Suite for Voltaire's Zaire)

Denham 28-29 December 1970	English Chamber Orchestra	LP: DG 2533 074

ADOLF HENSELT (1814-1889)

Piano Concerto in F minor

London 30 January- 1 February 1969	LSO Lewenthal	LP: CBS 61115/MG 35183

CHARLES MACKERRAS

· ROYAL · PHILHARMONIC ORCHESTRA

REZNICEK
OVERTURE "DONNA DIANA"

*

BURKHARD
OVERTURE "THE HUNTING PARSON"

*

"HIS MASTER'S VOICE"
EXTENDED PLAY 45 r.p.m. RECORD

(Photo: Derek Allen)

OVERTURE "IL SEGRETO DI SUSANNA," etc. ★ MACKERRAS **mono**

VICTOR HELY-HUTCHINSON (1901-1947)

The owl and the pussycat; The table and the chair; Old Mother Hubbard, arranged by Mackerras

London 11-12 January 1962	Pro Arte Orchestra Brannigan	LP: HMV CLP 1557/CSD 1437

VICTOR HERBERT (1859-1924)

Cello Concerto

London 21-22 April 1986	LSO Lloyd-Webber	LP: EMI EL 27 04301 CD: EMI CDC 747 6222

JOHANN HERTEL (1727-1789)

Trumpet Concerto in E flat

London 23-25 January 1977	English Chamber Orchestra André	LP: EMI ASD 3394/EG 29 04941/ 　　1C 065 02896/2C 069 02896 CD: EMI CDM 763 5282/CMS 769 8802

FRANZ HOFFMEISTER (1754-1812)

Flute Concerto in D

London 1978	English Chamber Orchestra Dingfelder	LP: Enigma ACM 2020 LP: Nonesuch H 71388 CD: ASV CDQS 6012

GUSTAV HOLST (1874-1934)

The Planets

Liverpool June 1988	Royal Liverpool PO and Chorus	CD: Virgin VJ 759 6452

The Perfect Fool, ballet suite

Liverpool June 1988	Royal Liverpool PO	CD: Virgin VJ 759 6452

CHARLES HORN (1786-1849)

Cherry ripe, arranged by Mackerras

London 26-27 April 1964	Pro Arte Orchestra Harwood	LP: EMI CLP 1789/CSD 1542/ESD 7002/ MFP 1014

ENGELBERT HUMPERDINCK (1854-1921)

Weihnachten, arranged by Mackerras

London 25 May- 1 July 1957	Philharmonia Orchestra & Chorus Schwarzkopf	LP: Columbia 33CX 1482 LP: Angel 35530/36750 LP: EMI ASD 3798/100 5431 CD: EMI CDM 763 5742

MIKHAIL IPPOLITOV-IVANOV (1859-1935)

Procession of the Sardar (Caucasian Sketches)

London 26 October 1956	Philharmonia	45: HMV 7EP 7084 LP: HMV DLP 1170 LP: Angel 35752

LEOS JANACEK (1854-1928)

Amarus, cantata

Prague 30 January 1984	Czech Philharmonic Orchestra & Chorus Nemeckova, Vodicka, Zitek	CD: Supraphon 1112 3576/30452/ C37-7735

The Ballad of Blanik, symphonic poem

London 24 July 1979	BBC SO	CD: Radio Classics 15656 91352

Capriccio for piano and chamber ensemble

Paris 11-13 June 1995	Members of Paris Opéra Orchestra Rudy	CD: EMI CDC 555 5852

Concertino for piano and chamber ensemble

Paris 11-13 June 1995	Members of Paris Opéra Orchestra Rudy	CD: EMI CDC 555 5852

The cunning little vixen

Vienna 13-26 March 1981	VPO Vienna Opera Chorus Popp, Randova, Krejeik, Jedlicka	LP: Decca D257 D2 LP: London LDR 72010 CD: Decca 417 1292
Paris 1996	Orchestre de Paris and Chorus Jenis, Marova, Hajna, Allen	Unpublished video recording

The cunning little vixen, concert suite arranged by Talich

Vienna 27 November 1979	VPO	CD: Decca 417 1292

Fate

Swansea July 1989	Welsh National Opera Orchestra and Chorus Field, Harries, Bronder, Langridge, Kale Sung in English	CD: EMI CDC 749 9932

From the house of the dead

Vienna 25 February- 5 March 1981	VPO Vienna Opera Chorus Blachut, Zidek, Zitek, Jedlicka	LP: Decca D224 D2 LP: London LDR 10036 CD: Decca 430 3752

From the house of the dead, prelude

Walthamstow 19-24 July 1959	Pro Arte Orchestra	LP: Pye CML 33007/GGC 4004/GSGC 14004/ GSGC 15033/GSGC 2018/71136

Glagolithic Mass

Prague 27-29 January 1984	Czech Philharmonic Orchestra & Chorus Söderström, Drobkova, Livora, Novak	CD: Supraphon 1112 3575/C37-7448
Copenhagen 21-24 January 1994	Danish Radio Orchestra & Chorus Kiberg, Stene, Svensson, Cold, Salo	CD: Chandos CHAN 9310 Original version

Jealousy, prelude (original prelude to Jenufa)

Walthamstow 19-24 July 1959	Pro Arte Orchestra	LP: Pye CML 33007/GGC 4004/GSGC 14004/ GSGC 15033/GSGC 2018/71136
Vienna 17-29 April 1902	VPO	LP: Decca D276 D3 LP: London LDR 73009

Jenufa

Vienna 17-29 April 1982	VPO Vienna Opera Chorus Söderström, Popp, Randova, Ochman, Dvorsky, Zitek	LP: Decca D276 D3 LP: London LDR 73009 CD: Decca 414 4832

Kata Kabanova

Vienna 1-14 December 1976	VPO Vienna Opera Chorus Söderström, Kniplova, Dvorsky, Krejcik, Jedlicka	LP: Decca D251 D2 LP: London OSA 12109 CD: Decca 421 8522
Prague March 1997	Czech PO and Chorus Benackova, Randova, Straka	CD: Supraphon awaiting publication

Kata Kabanova, prelude

Walthamstow 19-24 July 1959	Pro Arte Orchestra	LP: Pye CML 33007/GGC 4004/GSGC 14004/ GSGC 15033/GSGC 2018/71136

The Makropoulos Case

Vienna 25 September- 11 October 1978	VPO Vienna Opera Chorus Söderström, Dvorsky, Blachut, Krejcik, Zitek	LP: Decca D144 D2 LP: London OSA 12116 CD: Decca 430 3722

The Makropoulos Case, prelude

Walthamstow 19-24 July 1959	Pro Arte Orchestra	LP: Pye CML 33007/GGC 4004/GSGC 14004/ GSGC 15033/GSGC 2018/71136

Sinfonietta

Walthamstow 19-24 July 1959	Pro Arte Orchestra	LP: Pye CML 33007/GGC 4004/GSGC 14004/ GSGC 15033/GSGC 2018/71136
Vienna 26-27 November 1979	VPO	LP: Decca SXDL 7519 LP: London LDR 71021 CD: Decca 410 1382/430 7272/448 2552

Taras Bulba

Vienna 24-25 November 1979	VPO	LP: Decca SXDL 7519 LP: London LDR 71021 CD: Decca 410 1382/430 7272/ 440 9662/448 2552

ZOLTAN KODALY (1882-1967)

Psalmus hungaricus

Copenhagen 21-24 January 1994	Danish Radio Orchestra & Chorus Svensson	CD: Chandos CHAN 9310

EDOUARD LALO (1823-1892)

Cello Concerto

London 5-7 May 1976	New Philharmonia H.Schiff	LP: DG 2530 793 CD: DG 431 1662

LIZA LEHMANN (1862-1918)

Henry King (4 cautionary tales and a moral); Matilda, arranged by Mackerras

London 11-12 January 1962	Pro Arte Orchestra Brannigan	LP: HMV CLP 1557/CSD 1437

FRANZ LISZT (1811-1886)

Totentanz for piano and orchestra, arranged by Lewenthal

London 30 January- 1 February 1969	LSO Lewenthal	LP: CBS 61115/MG 35183

HENRY LITOLFF (1818-1891)

Scherzo (Concerto symphonique no 4)

Walthamstow 18-24 July 1959	Pro Arte Orchestra Cooper	45: Pye CEM 36015 LP: Pye CML 33006

GUSTAV MAHLER (1860-1911)

Symphony No 1

Liverpool 1-2 July 1991	Royal Liverpool PO	CD: EMI CDEMX 2197

Symphony No 4

London 4 May 1977	BBC SO Armstrong	CD: Radio Classics BBCRD 9101

Symphony No 5

Liverpool January 1990	Royal Liverpool PO	CD: EMI CDEMX 2164/CDB 572 1452

Des Knaben Wunderhorn, nos. 1-10, 13 and 14

London 16-21 October 1990	LPO Murray, Allen	CD: Virgin CUV 561 2022

BOHUSLAV MARTINU (1890-1959)

The Greek Passion

Brno 1-6 June 1981	Brno State PO Czech Philharmonic Chorus and Kuhn Chorus Field, Mitchinson, Tomlinson, Joll	LP: Supraphon 1116 3611-3612 CD: Supraphon 10.3611-3612 Excerpts CD: Koch 340362

Field Mass

Prague 20-21 January 1984	Czech Philharmonic Orchestra & Chorus Zitek	LP: Supraphon 1112 3576 CD: Supraphon C37-7735

Double Concerto for 2 string orchestras, piano and timpani

London 24 July 1979	BBC SO	CD: Radio Classics 15656 91352
Brno Date not confirmed	Brno State PO	CD: Conifer CDCF 202/CDCF 210
Prague 15-16 February 1982	Prague RO	LP: Supraphon 1110 3393 CD: Denon CO 1056

Les fresques de Piero della Francesca

Prague 15-16 February 1982	Prague RO	LP: Supraphon 1110 3393 CD: Denon CO 1056

Spalicek, ballet suite

Brno Not confirmed	Brno State PO	CD: Conifer CDCF 202

JULES MASSENET (1842-1912)

Manon, excerpts (Voice les élégants!/Suis-je gentille ainsi?/Je marche sur tous les chemins/Oui dans le bois)

London 22-27 May 1969	RPO Ambrosian Singers Sills, Fyson	LP: HMV ASD 2513/1C 063 90370/ 2C 069 90370 LP: ABC (USA) WST 17163

·Thaïs, Méditation

Walthamstow 21 July 1961	LSO	Mercury unpublished

FELIX MENDELSSOHN-BARTHOLDY (1809-1847)

Symphony No 4 "Italian"

London October 1987	Orchestra of the Age of Enlightenment	CD: Virgin VC 661 1832

Violin Concerto

Blackheath 20-21 October 1992	Orchestra of the Age of Enlightenment Huggett	CD: EMI CDEMX 2217/CDM 565 0272

A Midsummer Nights' Dream, excerpts from the incidental music

London October 1987	Orchestra of Age of Enlightenment	CD: Virgin CV 561 1832

ANDRE MESSAGER (1853-1929)

Les 2 pigeons, ballet music

London 25-28 April 1956	Philharmonia	LP: HMV CLP 1195 LP: EMI XLP 30022/SXLP 30022/CFP 40298 <u>Excerpts</u> LP: EMI ESDW 713

GIACOMO MEYERBEER (1791-1864)

Coronation March (Le prophète)

Walthamstow 21 July 1961	LSO	LP: Philips GL 5698/6747 204 LP: Philips (USA) PHM 500.105/ PHS 900.105 CD: Mercury 434 3522
London 12-14 April 1975	LPO	LP: Readers' Digest RDS 8024

Les Huguenots, excerpt (O beau pays de Touraine!)

London 22-27 May 1969	RPO Sills, Knibbs, Cable, Jennings	LP: EMI ASD 2513/1C 063 90370/ 2C 069 90370 LP: ABC (USA) WST 17163

Les patineurs, excerpts from the ballet arranged by Lambert

London 12 November 1958	Philharmonia	45: Columbia SED 5563/ESD 7254

Robert le diable, excerpt (Robert, toi que j'aime!)

London 22-27 May 1969	RPO Sills, Erwen	LP: EMI ASD 2513/1C 063 90370/ 2C 069 90370 LP: ABC (USA) WST 17163 CD: EMI CDC 747 1832

THOMAS MORLEY (1557-1602)

It was a lover and his lass

London	Pro Arte	LP: EMI CLP 1789/CSD 1542/ESD 7002/
26-27	Orchestra	MFP 1014
April	Harwood,	
1964	Brannigan	

WOLFGANG AMADEUS MOZART (1756-1791)

Unnumbered Symphonies K19a and K45b

Prague Prague CO CD: Telarc CD 80256/CD 80300
9-16
September
1990

Unnumbered Symphonies K81, K95 and K97

Prague Prague CO CD: Telarc CD 80272/CD 80300
9-16
September
1990

Unnumbered Symphonies K75 and K96

Prague Prague CO CD: Telarc CD 80273/CD 80300
9-16
September
1990

Symphonies 1, 4, 5, 6 and 7

Prague Prague CO CD: Telarc CD 80256/CD 80300
9-16
September
1990

Symphonies 8, 9 and 11

Prague Prague CO CD: Telarc CD 80272/CD 80300
9-16
September
1990

Symphonies 10, 12 and 13

Prague 9-16 September 1990	Prague CO	CD: Telarc CD 80273/CD 80300

Symphonies 14, 15, 16, 17 and 18

Prague 25-29 August 1989	Prague CO	CD: Telarc CD 80242/CD 80300

Symphonies 19, 20 and 21

Prague 25-29 August 1989	Prague CO	CD: Telarc CD 80217/CD 80300

Symphony No 22

Prague 25-29 August 1989	Prague CO	CD: Telarc CD 80217/CD 80300 CD: Supraphon 11 1186 2032

Symphony No 23

Prague 25-29 August 1989	Prague CO	CD: Telarc CD 80217/CD 80300 CD: Supraphon 11 1186 2032

Symphony No 24

Prague 10-17 July 1988	Prague CO	CD: Telarc CD 80186/CD 80300 CD: Supraphon 11 1186 2032

Symphony No 25

| Prague
1-7
July
1987 | Prague CO | CD: Telarc CD 80165/CD 80300
CD: Supraphon 11 1186 2032 |

Symphony No 26

| Prague
10-17
July
1988 | Prague CO | CD: Telarc CD 80186/CD 80300
CD: Supraphon 11 1186 2032 |

Symphony No 27

| Prague
10-17
July
1988 | Prague CO | CD: Telarc CD 80186/CD 80300
CD: Supraphon 11 1186 2032 |

Symphony No 28

| Prague
1-7
July
1987 | Prague CO | CD: Telarc CD 80165/CD 80300
CD: Supraphon 11 1186 2032 |

Symphony No 29

| Prague
1-7
July
1987 | Prague CO | CD: Telarc CD 80165/CD 80300
CD: Supraphon 11 1186 2032 |

Symphony No 30

| Prague
10-17
July
1988 | Prague CO | CD: Telarc CD 80186/CD 80300
CD: Supraphon 11 1186 2032 |

Symphony No 31 "Paris"

Prague 16 July 1989	Prague CO	CD: Telarc CD 80190/CD 80300 CD: Supraphon 11 1286 2031

Symphony No 32

London 26-27 January 1985	English Chamber Orchestra	LP: ASV DCA 543 CD: ASV CDQS 6071
Prague 10-17 July 1989	Prague CO	CD: Telarc CD 80203/CD 80300 CD: Supraphon 11 1497 2031

Symphony No 33

Prague 16 July 1989	Prague CO	CD: Telarc CD 80190/CD 80300 CD: Supraphon 11 1286 2031

Symphony No 34

Prague 16 July 1989	Prague CO	CD: Telarc CD 80190/CD 80300 CD: Supraphon 11 1286 2031

Symphony No 35 "Haffner"

London 26-27 January 1985	English Chamber Orchestra	LP: ASV DCA 543 CD: ASV CDQS 6071
Prague 10-17 July 1988	Prague CO	CD: Telarc CD 80203/CD 80300 CD: Supraphon 11 1497 2031

Symphony No 36 "Linz"

Barking 26-29 April 1973	LPO	LP: EMI CFP 40079/CFP 40336 CD: EMI CDCFPSD 4781/CMS 568 9662
Prague 12-14 June 1986	Prague CO	LP: Telarc DG 10138 CD: Telarc CD 80138/CD 80300 CD: Supraphon 11 07572

Symphony No 38 "Prague"

Barking 26-29 April 1973	LPO	LP: EMI CFP 40079/CFP 40336 CD: EMI CDCFPSD 4781/CMS 568 9662
Prague 12-14 June 1986	Prague CO	LP: Telarc DG 10138 CD: Telarc CD 80138/CD 80300 CD: Supraphon 11 07572

Symphony No 39

London 26-27 January 1985	English Chamber Orchestra	LP: ASV DCA 543 CD: ASV CDQS 6071
Prague 10-17 July 1988	Prague CO	CD: Telarc CD 80203/CD 80300

Symphony No 40

Barking 2-15 April 1975	LPO	LP: EMI CFP 40253 CD: EMI CDCFP 4253/CDB 769 9302
Prague 12-14 June 1986	Prague CO	LP: Telarc DG 10139 CD: Telarc CD 80139/CD 80300 CD: Supraphon 11 07572

Symphony No 41 "Jupiter"

Barking 2-15 April 1975	LPO	LP: EMI CFP 40253 CD: EMI CDCFP 4253/CDB 769 9302
Prague 12-14 June 1986	Prague CO	LP: Telarc DG 10139 CD: Telarc CD 80139/CD 80300 CD: Supraphon 11 07252

Piano Concerto No 17

Glasgow 28-29 October 1991	Scottish CO O'Conor	CD: Telarc CD 80306

Piano Concerto No 19

Edinburgh 4-5 September 1990	Scottish CO O'Conor	CD: Telarc CD 80285

Piano Concerto No 20

Barking 16-17 April 1975	LPO Schiller	LP: EMI CFP 40249 CD: EMI CDCFPSD 4781/CMS 568 9662
Glasgow 28-29 October 1991	Scottish CO O'Conor	CD: Telarc CD 80308

Piano Concerto No 21

Glasgow 4-5 September 1989	Scottish CO O'Conor	CD: Telarc CD 80219

Piano Concerto No 22

Glasgow 28-29 October 1991	Scottish CO O'Conor	CD: Telarc CD 80308

Piano Concerto No 23

Barking 16-17 April 1975	LPO Schiller	LP: EMI CFP 40249 CD: EMI CDCFPSD 4781/CMS 568 9662
Edinburgh 4-5 September 1990	Scottish CO O'Conor	CD: Telarc CD 80285

Piano Concerto No 24

Glasgow   Scottish CO   CD: Telarc CD 80306
28-29   O'Conor
October
1991

Piano Concerto No 27

Glasgow   Scottish CO   CD: Telarc CD 80219
4-5   O'Conor
September
1989

Concert rondo for piano and orchestra K386

Edinburgh   Scottish CO   CD: Telarc CD 80285
4-5   O'Conor
September
1990

Flute Concerto No 1

London   LPO   CD: EMI CDEMX 2181
20 November   Snowden
1990

Andante for flute and orchestra

London   LPO   EMI unpublished
20 November   Snowden
1990

The 4 Horn Concerti

Glasgow   Scottish CO   CD: Telarc CD 80367
4-5   Ruske
December
1993

Concert fragment for horn and orchestra

Glasgow 4-5 December 1993	Scottish CO Ruske	CD: Telarc CD 80367

Rondo for horn and orchestra

Glasgow 4-5 December 1993	Scottish CO Ruske	CD: Telarc CD 80367

Sinfonia concertante for wind

London 23-24 May 1991	LPO Theodore, Hill, Price, Busch	CD: EMI CDEMX 2181

Serenade No 6 "Serenata notturna"

Prague 1-7 July 1987	Prague CO	CD: Telarc CD 80161 CD: Supraphon 11 0778 2031

Serenade No 7 "Haffner"

Prague 1-7 July 1987	Prague CO	CD: Telarc CD 80161 CD: Supraphon 11 0778 2031

Serenade No 9 "Posthorn"

Prague 3-7 October 1984	Prague CO	LP: Telarc DG 10108 CD: Telarc CD 80108 CD: Supraphon 10 4145 2031

Serenade No 10 for 13 wind instruments

Purchase NY 1-2 July 1993	Orchestra of St Lukes	CD: Telarc CD 80359

Serenade No 13 "Eine kleine Nachtmusik"

Prague 3-7 October 1984	Prague CO	LP: Telarc DG 10108 CD: Telarc CD 80108 CD: Supraphon 10 4145 2031

Divertimento No 1 for wind and strings

Walthamstow 18 July 1959	Pro Arte Orchestra	LP: Pye GGC 4033/GSGC 14033 LP: Vanguard SRV 186

Les petits riens, ballet music

Walthamstow 18 July 1959	Pro Arte Orchestra	LP: Pye GGC 4033/GSGC 14033 LP: Vanguard SRV 186

6 German dances K600

Walthamstow 18 July 1959	Pro Arte Orchestra	LP: Pye GGC 4033/GSGC 14033 LP: Vanguard SRV 186

2 Marches K408

Walthamstow 18 July 1959	Pro Arte Orchestra	LP: Pye GGC 4033/GSGC 14033 LP: Vanguard SRV 186

2 Minuets K604

Walthamstow	Pro Arte	LP: Pye GGC 4033/GSGC 14033
18 July	Orchestra	LP: Vanguard SRV 186
1959		

Ah se in ciel benigne stelle, concert aria

Munich	Bavarian RO	LP: DG LPEM 18 183/SLPEM 136 028/
22-29	Streich	2535 465
September		CD: DG 431 8752
1958		

Chi sa chi sa qual sia, concert aria

Cardiff	Welsh National	VHS Video: EMI MVC 991 2423
19 March	Opera Orchestra	Laserdisc: EMI LDA 991 2421
1990	Kanawa	

La clemenza di Tito, overture

Cardiff	Welsh National	VHS Video: EMI MVC 991 2423
19 March	Opera Orchestra	Laserdisc: EMI LDA 991 2421
1990		

La clemenza di Tito, excerpt (Se all' impero)

Cardiff	Welsh National	VHS Video: EMI MVC 991 2423
19 March	Opera Orchestra	Laserdisc: EMI LDA 991 2421
1990	Kanawa	

Così fan tutte

Edinburgh 2-13 August 1993	Scottish CO Edinburgh Festival Chorus Lott, McLaughlin, Focile, Hadley, Corbelli, Cachemaille	CD: Telarc CD 80360 <u>Excerpts</u> CD: Telarc CD 80399

Don Giovanni

Edinburgh 31 July- 11 August 1995	Scottish CO Edinburgh Festival Chorus Lott, Brewer, Focile, Hadley, Skovhus, Corbelli, Chiummo	CD: Telarc CD 80420 <u>Excerpts</u> CD: Telarc CD 80446 <u>This recording includes most of</u> <u>the music for both Prague and</u> <u>Vienna versions of the opera as</u> <u>well as concert version of the</u> <u>overture as an appendix</u>

Don Giovanni, excerpt (Ah fuggi il traditor!)

Cardiff 19 March 1990	Welsh National Opera Orchestra Kanawa	VHS Video: EMI MVC 991 2423 Laserdisc: EMI LDA 991 2421

Die Entführung aus dem Serail, excerpt (Ach, ich liebte)

New York December 1995	Orchestra of St Lukes Fleming	CD: Decca 452 6022

Exsultate jubilate

Cardiff 19 March 1990	Welsh National Opera Orchestra Kanawa	VHS Video: EMI MVC 991 2423 Laserdisc: EMI LDA 991 2421

La finta giardiniera, excerpts (Geme la tortorella; Crudeli fermate, o Dio, fermate!; Ah dal pianto dal singhiozzo)

New York December 1995	Orchestra of St Lukes Fleming	CD: Decca 452 6022

Mia speranza adorata, concert aria

Munich 22-29 September 1958	Bavarian RO Streich	LP: DG LPEM 19 183/SLPEM 136 028/ 2535 465 CD: DG 431 8752

Nehmt meinen Dank, concert aria

Munich 22-29 September 1958	Bavarian RO Streich	LP: DG LPEM 19 183/SLPEM 136 028/ 2535 465 CD: DG 431 8752
Cardiff 19 March 1990	Welsh National Opera Orchestra Kanawa	VHS Video: EMI MVC 991 2423 Laserdisc: EMI LDA 991 2421
New York December 1995	Orchestra of St Lukes Fleming	CD: Decca 452 6022

No che non sei capace, concert aria

Munich 22-29 September 1958	Bavarian RO Streich	LP: DG LPEM 19 183/SLPEM 136 028/ 2535 465 CD: DG 431 8752

Non so d'onde viene, concert aria

Munich 22-29 September 1958	Bavarian RO Streich	LP: DG LPEM 19 183/SLPEM 136 028/ 2535 465 CD: DG 431 8752

LE NOZZE DI FIGARO

Opera buffa in four acts by
W A MOZART

Libretto by
LORENZO DA PONTE
after *Le Mariage de Figaro* by BEAUMARCHAIS

Sung in Italian with English supertitles

Conductor	CHARLES MACKERRAS
	CHRISTOPHER MOULDS *(July 5)*
Director	STEPHEN MEDCALF
Designer	JOHN GUNTER
Lighting Designer	KEITH BENSON
Choreographer	JENNY WESTON
Assistant Director	ROBIN MARTIN-OLIVER

Cast

Figaro	ANTON SCHARINGER
Susanna	ROSEMARY JOSHUA
Bartolo	ENRICO FISSORE
Marcellina	SUSAN MCCULLOCH
Cherubino	SUSANNAH WATERS
Don Basilio	RYLAND DAVIES
Count Almaviva	WOJCIECH DRABOWICZ
Countess Almaviva	NORAH AMSELLEM
Antonio	HENRY WADDINGTON
Don Curzio	RYLAND DAVIES
Barbarina	LINDA TUVÅS
Bridesmaid	EMMA POLLARD
Harpsichord continuo	IAN PAGE
Cello continuo	SUSANNE BEER

LONDON PHILHARMONIC ORCHESTRA
THE GLYNDEBOURNE CHORUS

Performances on June 7, 12, 14, 19, 22, 26, 29, July 5, 8, 11, 13, 16, 21, 25, 28
Curtain up 5pm Dinner Interval 6.50pm Curtain down 9.55pm approximately Sundays one hour and fifteen minutes earlier
First performed in Vienna, 1.V.1786
First performed at Glyndebourne, 28.V.1934
First performance of this production at Glyndebourne, 28.V.1994

Glyndebourne Festival 1997

Le nozze di Figaro

Edinburgh 31 July- 12 August 1994	Scottish CO Edinburgh Festival Chorus Vaness, Focile, Mentzer, Miles, Corbelli	CD: Telarc CD 80388

Le nozze di Figaro, overture

Cardiff 19 March 1990	Welsh National Opera Orchestra	VHS Video: EMI MVC 991 2423 Laserdisc: EMI LDA 991 2421

Le nozze di Figaro, excerpts (Porgi amor; Dove sono)

Cardiff 19 March 1990	Welsh National Opera Orchestra Kanawa	VHS Video: EMI MVC 991 2423 Laserdisc: EMI LDA 991 2421

Le nozze di Figaro, excerpt (Deh vieni non tardar)

New York December 1995	Orchestra of St Lukes Fleming	CD: Decca 452 6022

Le nozze di Figaro, excerpt (Al desio/alternative version of Deh vieni non tardar)

New York December 1995	Orchestra of St Lukes Fleming	CD: Decca 452 6022

Popoli di Tessaglia, concert aria

Munich 22-29 September 1958	Bavarian RO Streich	LP: DG LPEM 19 183/SLPEM 136 028/ 2535 465 CD: DG 431 8752

Il rè pastore, excerpt (L'amerò sarò costante)

New York December 1995	Orchestra of St Lukes Fleming	CD: Decca 452 6022

Il sogno di Scipione, excerpt (Lieve son al par del vento)

New York December 1995	Orchestra of St Lukes Fleming	CD: Decca 452 6022

Vado ma dove?, concert aria

Munich 22-29 September 1958	Bavarian RO Streich	LP: DG LPEM 19 183/SLPEM 136 028/ 2535 465 CD: DG 431 8752
Cardiff 19 March 1990	Welsh National Opera Orchestra Kanawa	VHS Video: EMI MVC 991 2423 Laserdisc: EMI LDA 991 2421

Vorrei spiegarvi o Dio!, concert aria

Munich 22-29 September 1958	Bavarian RO Streich	LP: DG LPEM 19 183/SLPEM 136 028/ 2535 465 CD: DG 431 8752

Zaide, excerpt (Ruhe sanft, mein holdes Leben)

New York December 1995	Orchestra of St Lukes Fleming	CD: Decca 452 6022

Die Zauberflöte

Edinburgh 13-22 July 1991	Scottish CO Edinburgh Festival Chorus Hendricks, Anderson, Hadley, Allen, Lloyd, Hornik	CD: Telarc CD 80302 <u>Excerpts</u> CD: Telarc CD 80345/CD 80407

Die Zauberflöte, excerpt (Ach, ich fühl's)

Cardiff 19 March 1990	Welsh National Opera Orchestra Kanawa	VHS Video: EMI MVC 991 2423 Laserdisc: EMI LDA 991 2421
New York December 1995	Orchestra of St Lukes Fleming	CD: Decca 452 6022

MODEST MUSSORGSKY (1839-1881)

Pictures from an exhibition, arranged by Ravel

London 13 July 1974	New Philharmonia	LP: Vanguard 71180/VCS 10116/VS24-25 CD: Vanguard 08.406571
Liverpool January 1990	Royal Liverpool PO	CD: Virgin VC 759 6252

Night on Bare Mountain, arranged by Rimsky-Korsakov

Barking 4-15 June 1970	LPO	LP: EMI CFP 101 CD: EMI CDCFP 9000
Liverpool January 1990	Royal Liverpool PO	CD: Virgin CUV 561 1352/VC 759 6252

Khovantschina, prelude

London 13 July 1974	New Philharmonia	LP: Vanguard 71180/VCS 10116

Gopak (Sorochinsky Fair), arranged by Liadov

London 25 October 1956	Philharmonia	45: HMV 7EP 7084 LP: HMV DLP 1170 CD: EMI CZS 568 5502

OTTO NICOLAI (1810-1849)

Die lustigen Weiber von Windsor, overture

Walthamstow 19 July 1961	LSO	LP: Philips GL 5698/DAL 502/SDAL 502 LP: Philips (USA) PHM 500.022/ PHS 900.022 CD: Mercury 434 3522

JACQUES OFFENBACH (1819-1880)

Gaîté parisienne, ballet suite arranged by Rosenthal

London	Philharmonia	LP: HMV CLP 1722/CSD 1533
8-9		LP: Capitol P 8654/SP 8654
May		LP: EMI XLP 30011/SXLP 30011/CFP 40268
1961		LP: Arabesque 8020

Orfée aux enfers, overture arranged by André

Walthamstow	LSO	LP: Philips GL 5698/DAL 502/SDAL 502
23 July		LP: Philips (USA) PHM 500.022/
1961		PHS 900.022
		CD: Mercury 434 3522

Orfée aux enfers, Can-can

Walthamstow	LSO	LP: Philips (USA) PHM 500.105/
21-22		PHS 900.105
July		CD: Mercury 434 3522
1961		

AMILCARE PONCHIELLI (1834-1886)

Dance of the hours (La gioconda)

London	Philharmonia	LP: Columbia 33SX 1207/SCX 3291
12 November		LP: Angel 35833
1958		LP: EMI MFP 2085/ESD 7115

SERGEI PROKOFIEV (1891-1953)

Peter and the Wolf

London	LSO	CD: Cala CACD 1022
1994	Kingsley	

GIACOMO PUCCINI (1858-1924)

La Bohème, excerpts (Sì mi chiamano Mimì; Donde lieta uscì)

London 31 March- 10 April 1970	LSO Caballé	LP: EMI ASD 2632/SXLP 30562/ 1C 037 02099 LP: Angel 36711 CD: EMI CDC 747 8412

Gianni Schicchi, excerpt (O mio babbino caro)

London 31 March- 10 April 1970	LSO Caballé	LP: EMI ASD 2632/SXLP 30562/ 1C 037 02099 LP: Angel 36711 CD: EMI CDC 747 8412

Madama Butterfly, excerpts (Un bel dì; Tu tu piccolo iddio!)

London 31 March- 10 April 1970	LSO Caballé	LP: EMI ASD 2632/SXLP 30562/ 1C 037 02099 LP: Angel 36711 CD: EMI CDC 747 8412

Manon Lescaut, excerpts (In quelle trine morbide; Sola perduta abbandonata)

London 31 March- 10 April 1970	LSO Caballé	LP: EMI ASD 2632/SXLP 30562/ 1C 037 02099 LP: Angel 36711 CD: EMI CDC 747 8412

Manon Lescaut, excerpt (Tu tu amore!)

London 31 March- 10 April 1970	LSO Caballé, Marti	LP: EMI ASD 2723

La fanciulla del West, excerpt (Laggiù nel Soledad)

Hamburg 1976	Philharmonisches Staatsorchester Silja, Janulako <u>Sung in German</u>	LP: Legendary LR 131

La rondine, excerpt (Che il bel sogno)

London	LSO	LP: EMI ASD 2632/SXLP 30562/
31 March-	Caballé	1C 037 02099
10 April		LP: Angel 36711
1970		CD: EMI CDC 747 8412

Tosca, excerpt (Vissi d'arte)

London	LSO	LP: EMI ASD 2632/SXLP 30562/
31 March-	Caballé	1C 037 02099
10 April		LP: Angel 36711
1970		CD: EMI CDC 747 8412

Turandot, excerpts (Signore ascolta!; Tu che di gel sei cinta)

London	LSO	LP: EMI ASD 2632/SXLP 30562/
31 March-	Caballé	1C 037 02099
10 April		LP: Angel 36711
1970		CD: EMI CDC 747 8412

Le villi, excerpt (Se come voi piccina)

London	LSO	LP: EMI ASD 2632/SXLP 30562/
31 March-	Caballé	1C 037 02099
10 April		LP: Angel 36711
1970		CD: EMI CDC 747 8412

HENRY PURCELL (1659-1695)

Dido and Aeneas

Hamburg 30 September- 4 October 1967	NDR Orchestra Monteverdi Choir Troyanos, Armstrong, Johnson, McDaniel	LP: DG SAPM 198 424/2547 032 CD: DG 447 1482 Excerpts CD: DG 439 4742

The Indian Queen, incidental music

London 1-2 November 1965	English Chamber Orchestra St Anthony Singers Cantelo, Brown, Tear, Partridge, Keyte	LP: Decca OL 294/SOL 294/410 7161 CD: Decca 433 1662

Ode on St Cecilia's Day "Hail, bright Cecilia!"

Wembley 9-11 January 1969	English Chamber Orchestra Ambrosian Singers Wolff, Esswood, Tatnell, Young, Shirley-Quirk, Rippon	LP: DG 2533 042 CD: DG 447 1492

SERGEI RACHMANINOV (1873-1943)

Symphony No 3

Liverpool April 1989	Royal Liverpool PO	CD: EMI CDCFP 4649

Symphonic dances

Liverpool April 1989	Royal Liverpool PO	CD: EMI CDCFP 4649

JEAN-PHILIPPE RAMEAU (1683-1764)

Castor et Pollux, ballet suite

Walthamstow 19-23 July 1961	LSO	LP: Westminster WS 9002

MAURICE RAVEL (1875-1937)

Daphnis et Chloé, Second suite

London August 1980	LSO	LP: Centaur CRC 1007

MAX REGER (1873-1916)

An die Hoffnung

London 10 July 1966	New Philharmonia C.Ludwig	EMI unpublished

EMIL VON REZNICEK (1860-1945)

Donna Diana, overture

London 4 June 1956	RPO	45: HMV 7EP 7037

OTTORINO RESPIGHI (1879-1936)

Trittico botticelliano

Walthamstow 8 February 1969	LSO	CD: Radio Classics 15656 91372

NIKOLAI RIMSKY-KORSAKOV (1844-1908)

Scheherazade

Walthamstow 12-14 March 1990	LSO	CD: Telarc CD 80208

Capriccio espagnol

Walthamstow 12-14 March 1990	LSO	CD: Telarc CD 80208

Dance of the tumblers (The Snow Maiden)

London 26 October 1956	Philharmonia	45: HMV 7EP 7084 LP: HMV DLP 1170 LP: Angel 35752

Flight of the bumble bee (Tsar Sultan)

London 25 October 1956	Philharmonia	45: HMV 7EP 7084 LP: HMV DLP 1170

March (Le coq d'or)

London 12-14 April 1975	LPO	LP: Readers' Digest RDS 8024

GIOACHINO ROSSINI (1792-1868)

Guillaume Tell, ballet music

London 8-9 May 1968	New Philharmonia	LP: EMI TWO 275/CFP 40229 LP: Angel 60284

CAMILLE SAINT-SAENS (1835-1921)

Cello Concerto No 1

London 5-7 May 1976	New Philharmonia H.Schiff	LP: DG 2530 793 CD: DG 431 1662

Introduction and rondo capriccioso for violin and orchestra

London 27 April- 18 May 1969	LSO Zukerman	LP: CBS MS 7422/72828 CD: Sony SBK 48270

Wedding Cake Caprice for piano and orchestra

Walthamstow 18-24 July 1959	Pro Arte Orchestra Cooper	45: Pye CEM 36015

DOMENICO SCARLATTI (1685-1757)

Stabat mater

Paris 1-7 October 1975	Kuentz Chamber Orchestra Freni, Berganza	LP: DG 2533 324

FRANZ SCHUBERT (1797-1828)

Symphony No 5

London November 1990	Orchestra of the Age of Enlightenment	CD: Virgin VC 759 2732

Symphony No 8 "Unfinished"

London November 1990	Orchestra of the Age of Enlightenment	CD: Virgin VC 759 2732

Symphony No 9 "Great"

London October 1987	Orchestra of the Age of Enlightenment	CD: Virgin VC 759 6692

Symphony No 10, arranged by Newbould

Glasgow 1996	Scottish CO	CD: Hyperion CDA 67000 <u>CD also contains realisation of other Schubert symphonic fragments</u>

Rosamunde, Entr'acte in B minor and Ballet in G

London November 1990	Orchestra of the Age of Enlightenment	CD: Virgin VC 759 2732

DIMITRI SHOSTAKOVICH (1906-1975)

Violin Concerto No 1

Prague 1982	Prague RO Tomasek	CD: Praga PR 250052

JEAN SIBELIUS (1865-1957)

Symphony No 2

London 5-6 July 1988	LSO	CD: LSO Classics PCD 927 <u>Fourth movement</u> CD: IMP PCDS 24
London January 1994	RPO	CD: Tring TRPO 13

Finlandia

Walthamstow 27-30 May 1958	LSO	LP: Victor LM 2336/LSC 2336/RB 16179/ SB 2069/VIC 1069/VICS 1069 LP: Decca SPA 91/DPA 511-512 LP: London STS 15159
London January 1994	RPO	CD: Tring TRPO 13

Karelia suite

London January 1994	RPO	CD: Tring TRPO 13

Karelia, Alla marcia

London 12-14 April 1975	LPO	LP: Readers' Digest RDS 8024

King Christian II, Elégie and musette

Walthamstow 27-30 May 1958	LSO	LP: Victor LM 2336/LSC 2336/RB 16179/ SB 2069/VIC 1069/VICS 1069 LP: Decca SPA 91 LP: London STS 15159

Pelleas and Melisande, entr'acte

Walthamstow 27-30 May 1958	LSO	LP: Victor LM 2336/LSC 2336/RB 16179/ SB 2069/VIC 1069/VICS 1069 LP: Decca SPA 91 LP: London STS 15159

The Swan of Tuonela

London 5-6 July 1988	LSO	CD: LSO Classics PCD 927

Valse triste

Walthamstow 27-30 May 1958	LSO	LP: Victor LM 2336/LSC 2336/RB 16179/ SB 2069/VIC 1069/VICS 1069 LP: Decca SPA 91/VIV 44 LP: London STS 15159

SITSKY

Concerto for wind quintet and orchestra

Sydney 23 April 1971	Sydney SO and Wind Quintet	LP: ABC/World Records (Australia) RO 4694

BEDRICH SMETANA (1824-1884)

The Bartered Bride, overture

Walthamstow 18-24 July 1959	Pro Arte Orchestra	45: Pye CEM 36014/CSEM 75007 LP: Pye GGC 4011/GSGC 14011 LP: Vanguard SRV 178

The Bartered Bride, polka and furiant

London 31 October 1960	Philharmonia	45: Columbia SED 5578/ESD 7268 LP: Columbia 33SX 1389/SCX 3427 LP: EMI CFP 40214

The Bartered Bride, Dance of the Comedians

Walthamstow 23 July 1961	LSO	LP: Philips GL 5698/6747 050 LP: Philips (USA) PHM 500.022/ PHS 900.022 CD: Mercury 434 3522

OLEY SPEAKS (1874-1948)

Mandalay scena

London 4 May 1955	LSO Dawson	45: HMV 7EG 8157 LP: HMV (Australia) PD 1 <u>Additional composers probably involved in this composition</u>

GOTTFRIED STOELZEL (1670-1749)

Trumpet Concerto in D

London 22-23 May 1976	English Chamber Orchestra André	LP: DG 2530 792/410 8321

JOHANN STRAUSS I (1804-1849)

Radetzky march

Walthamstow 21 July 1961	LSO	LP: Philips GL 5698/6747 071 LP: Philips (USA) PHM 500.105/ PHS 900.105 CD: Mercury 434 3522

JOHANN STRAUSS II (1825-1899)

Graduation Ball, ballet arranged by Dorati

London 17 April– 9 May 1961	Philharmonia	LP: HMV CLP 1722/CSD 1533 LP: Capitol P 8654/SP 8654 LP: EMI XLP 30011/SXLP 30011/CFP 40268 LP: Arabesque 8020

RICHARD STRAUSS (1864-1949)

Don Juan

Barking 15 January 1973	LPO	LP: EMI CFP 40042/CFP 40307

Till Eulenspiegels lustige Streiche

Barking 15 January 1973	LPO	LP: EMI CFP 40042/CFP 40307

IGOR STRAVINSKY (1882-1971)

Circus polka

Watford 30 August– 1 September 1987	LPO	LP: EMI EMX 2188 CD: EMI CDEMX 2188

Fireworks

Watford 30 August– 1 September 1987	LPO	LP: EMI EMX 2188 CD: EMI CDEMX 2188

Greeting prelude

Watford 30 August– 1 September 1987	LPO	LP: EMI EMX 2188 CD: EMI CDEMX 2188

Petrushka, 1911 version

Watford 23 July 1972	LSO	LP: Vanguard VSD 71137/VCS 10113/ VSQ 30021 CD: Vanguard 08.406571

Le sacre du printemps

Watford 30 August– 1 September 1987	LPO	LP: EMI EMX 2188 CD: EMI CDEMX 2188

ARTHUR SULLIVAN (1842-1900)

Cello Concerto

London 21-22 April 1986	LSO Lloyd-Webber	LP: EMI EL 27 04301 CD: EMI CDC 747 6222/CDM 764 7262

Di ballo, overture

London 26-27 November 1982	Philharmonia	LP: Decca SXDL 7619 LP: London LDR 71119 CD: Decca 436 8132

Iolanthe, overture

London 9 June 1956	Philharmonia	45: HMV 7EP 7037/PES 5254 CD: EMI CDM 566 5382

The Mikado

Swansea 2-4 September 1991	Welsh National Opera Orchestra and Chorus McLaughlin, Howells, Palmer, Rolfe-Johnson, Adams, Suart, Folwell	CD: Telarc CD 80284 Recording without dialogue Excerpts CD: Telarc CD 80431

The Mikado, overture

London 9 June 1956	Philharmonia	LP: EMI CFP 40279 CD: EMI CDM 566 5382

The Pirates of Penzance

Swansea 4-6 May 1993	Welsh National Opera Orchestra and Chorus R.Evans, Knight, Ainsley, Adams, Suart, Folwell, Van Allan	CD: Telarc CD 80353 Recording without dialogue Excerpts CD: Telarc CD 80431

Pineapple Poll, ballet arranged by Mackerras

London 7-8 June 1951	Sadlers Wells Orchestra	78: Columbia DX 1765-1770 LP: Columbia 33SX 1001
London 3-5 October 1960	RPO	LP: HMV CLP 1494/CSD 1399 LP: Capitol P 8663/SP 8663 LP: EMI ESD 7028 LP: Arabesque 8016 CD: Arabesque Z 8016 CD: EMI CDM 566 5382
London 26-27 March 1977	LPO	LP: EMI CFP 40293/CFP 41 44901 CD: EMI CDCFP 4618 This recording is of excerpts only
London 26-27 November 1982	Philharmonia	LP: Decca SXDL 7619 LP: London LDR 71119 CD: Decca 436 8102

HMS Pinafore

Swansea 5-8 June 1994	Welsh National Opera Orchestra and Chorus R.Evans, Palmer, Schade, Adams, Suart, Van Allan	CD: Telarc CD 80374 Recording without dialogue Excerpts CD: Telarc CD 80431

Ruddigore, overture

London 9 June 1956	Philharmonia	45: HMV 7EP 7037/PES 5254 LP: EMI CFP 40279 CD: EMI CDM 566 5382

Trial by Jury

Swansea 1995	Welsh National Opera Orchestra and Chorus R.Evans, Banks, Suart, Savidge, Adams	CD: Telarc CD 80404 <u>Excerpts</u> CD: Telarc CD 80431

The Yeomen of the Guard

Swansea 1995	Welsh National Opera Orchestra and Chorus Stephen, Mellor, C.O'Neill, Palmer, Archer, Hoare, Suart, Savidge, Adams, Maxwell	CD: Telarc CD 80404 <u>Excerpts</u> CD: Telarc CD 80431

The Yeomen of the Guard, overture

London 9 June 1956	Philharmonia	CD: EMI CDM 566 5382

FRANZ VON SUPPE (1818-1895)

Banditenstreiche, overture

Walthamstow 23 July 1961	LSO	LP: Philips (USA) PHM 500.105/ PHS 900.105 CD: Mercury 434 3522

DONALD SWANN (1923-1994)

III Wind, song after Mozart's Horn Concerto No 4

Edinburgh 4-5 December 1993	Scottish CO Suart	CD: Telarc CD 80367

PIOTR TCHAIKOVSKY (1840-1893)

Symphony No 4

Hamburg 14-18 May 1967	Philharmonisches Staatsorchester	LP: Checkmate (USA) 76004

Symphony No 5, third movement

London 1 July 1958	Philharmonia	45: Columbia SED 5564/ESD 7252 LP: Angel 35752

Symphony No 6 "Pathétique"

Hamburg 14-18 May 1967	Philharmonisches Staatsorchester	LP: Checkmate (USA) 76009

Piano Concerto No 3

Walthamstow 18-24 July 1959	Pro Arte Orchestra Cooper	LP: Pye CML 33006

1812 Overture

Barking 4-15 June 1970	LPO	LP: EMI CFP 101

Marche slave

London 12-14 August 1975	LPO	LP: Readers' Digest RDS 8024

Rococo Variations for cello and orchestra

London	LPO	CD: RCA/BMG RD 60758
31 December	Harnoy	
1990		

Andante cantabile for cello and orchestra

London	LPO	CD: RCA/BMG RD 60758
23-24	Harnoy	
November		
1990		

Nocturne for cello and orchestra

London	LPO	CD: RCA/BMG RD 60758
31 December	Harnoy	
1990		

Pezzo capriccioso for cello and orchestra

London	LPO	CD: RCA/BMG RD 60758
25 November	Harnoy	
1990		

Sérénade mélancolique, arranged for cello and orchestra by J.Harnoy

London	LPO	CD: RCA/BMG RD 60758
23-24	Harnoy	
November		
1990		

October (The Seasons), arranged for cello and orchestra by J.Harnoy

London	LPO	CD: RCA/BMG RD 60758
31 December	Harnoy	
1990		

Valse sentimentale (Morceaux), arranged for cello and orchestra by J.Harnoy

London 23-24 November 1990	LPO Harnoy	CD: RCA/BMG RD 60758

Casse noisette

Watford 13-16 May 1986	LSO	LP: Telarc DG 10137 CD: Telarc CD 80137 <u>Excerpts</u> CD: Telarc CD 80140

Casse noisette, Valse des fleurs

London 1 July 1958	Philharmonia	45: Columbia SED 5564/ESD 7252 LP: Angel 35752

Evgeny Onegin

Swansea June-July 1992	Welsh National Opera Orchestra and Chorus Kanawa, Bardon, Finnie, Rosenshein, Gedda, Hampson, J.Connell <u>Sung in English</u>	CD: EMI CDS 565 0042 <u>Excerpts</u> CD: EMI CDM 565 5782

Evgeny Onegin, Lensky's aria arranged for cello and orchestra by J.Harnoy

London 23-24 November 1990	LPO Harnoy	CD: RCA/BMG RD 60758

Evgeny Onegin, waltz

London 1 July 1958	Philharmonia	45: Columbia SED 5566/ESD 7258 LP: Angel 35752

Mazeppa, Cossack dance

Walthamstow
22 July
1961
	LSO	LP: Philips GL 5698/6747 050/6747 056/
		    6747 327/6833 032
		LP: Philips (USA) PHM 500.022/
		    PHS 900.022
		CD: Mercury 434 3522

Pique Dame, duet of Daphnis and Chloe

Watford 13-16 May 1986	LSO	LP: Telarc DG 10137 CD: Telarc CD 80137

The Sleeping Beauty, ballet suite

Watford 30-31 March 1987	RPO	CD: Telarc CD 80151

The Sleeping Beauty, waltz

London 1 July 1958	Philharmonia	Columbia unpublished

Swan Lake, ballet suite

Watford 30-31 March 1987	RPO	CD: Telarc CD 80151

Swan Lake, waltz

London 1 July 1958	Philharmonia	45: Columbia SED 5566/ESD 7258 LP: Angel 35752

SADLER'S WELLS

Re-opened by LILIAN BAYLIS, January 6th, 1931

OPERA
AND
BALLET

FESTIVAL SEASON
1951

MONDAY EVENING AUGUST 27th 1951

The Barber of Seville

A Comic Opera in Three Acts by ROSSINI
(English Translation by Edward J. Dent)

Conductor : CHARLES MACKERRAS

Producer : TYRONE GUTHRIE
Designer : RUTH KEATING

Characters

Fiorello, *Servant to Count Almaviva*	CECIL LLOYD
Count Almaviva	JOHN KENTISH
Figaro, *a Barber*	DENIS DOWLING
Rosina, *the Rich Ward of Dr. Bartolo*	MARJORIE SHIRES
Dr. Bartolo	GEORGE JAMES
Marcellina, *his Housekeeper*	OLWEN PRICE
Ambrogio, *his Manservant*	LEON HOCHLOFF
Don Basilio, *Rosina's Music Master*	HERVEY ALAN
Sergeant	DESMOND D'ARCY
Notary	IVOR INGHAM
Alcalde	CHARLES DRAPER

GEORG PHILIPP TELEMANN (1681-1767)

Concerto for trumpet, oboes and strings, arranged by Grebe

| London
23-25
January
1977 | English Chamber
Orchestra
André | LP: EMI ASD 3394/EG 29 04941/
     1C 065 02896/2C 069 02896
CD: EMI CDM 763 5282/CMS 769 8802/
    CZS 767 8942 |

Sonata in D for trumpet and strings

| London
22-23
May
1976 | English Chamber
Orchestra
André | LP: DG 2530 792/410 8321
CD: DG 413 8532/415 9802/419 8742 |

AMBROISE THOMAS (1811-1896)

Hamlet, excerpt (A vos jeux!/Partagez-vous mes fleurs!)

| London
22-27
May
1969 | RPO
Sills | LP: EMI ASD 2513/1C 063 90370/
    2C 069 90370
LP: ABC (USA) WST 17163/ATS 20019
LP: Angel 34016 |

Mignon, excerpt (Je suis Titania!)

| London
22-27
May
1969 | RPO
Sills | LP: EMI ASD 2513/1C 063 90370/
    2C 069 90370
LP: ABC (USA) WST 17163 |

Mignon, overture

| Walthamstow
23 July
1961 | LSO | LP: Philips (USA) PHM 500.105/
    PHS 900.105
CD: Mercury 434 3522 |

GIUSEPPE TORELLI (1658-1709)

Trumpet Concerto in D

London 22-23 May 1976	English Chamber Orchestra	LP: DG 2530 792/410 8321 CD: DG 413 8532

GEOFFREY TOYE (1889-1942)

The Haunted Ballroom, concert waltz

London 10-11 July 1951	Sadlers Wells Orchestra	Columbia unpublished

JOAQUIN TURINA (1882-1949)

Rapsodia sinfonica

Walthamstow 18-24 July 1959	Pro Arte Orchestra Cooper	LP: Pye CML 33006

GIUSEPPE VERDI (1813-1901)

Alzira, overture

London 2-3 November 1956	Philharmonia	45: HMV 7EP 7080 LP: HMV DLP 1185 LP: Angel 35751/60354 LP: EMI XLP 30019/SXLP 30019

Un ballo in maschera

San Francisco 1971	San Francisco Opera Orchestra and Chorus Arroyo, Donath, Dalis, Pavarotti, Bordin	CD: Butterfly BMCD 022

Un ballo in maschera, excerpt (Teco io sto)

London 31 March- 10 April 1970	LSO Caballé, Marti	LP: EMI ASD 2723

La forza del destino, overture

London 2-3 November 1956	Philharmonia	LP: HMV DLP 1185 LP: Angel 35751/60354 LP: EMI XLP 30019/SXLP 30019

The Lady and the Fool, ballet arranged by Mackerras

London 21-30 June 1955	Philharmonia	LP: HMV CLP 1059/XLP 30006 Excerpts 45: HMV 7ER 7081
London 26-27 March 1977	LPO	LP: EMI CFP 40293/CFP 41 44901 CD: EMI CDCFP 4618 This version is of excerpts only

Luisa Miller, overture

London 2-3 November 1956	Philharmonia	45: HMV 7EP 7080 LP: HMV DLP 1185 LP: Angel 35751/60354 LP: EMI XLP 30019/SXLP 30019

Nabucco, overture

London 2-3 November 1956	Philharmonia	LP: HMV DLP 1185 LP: Angel 35751/60354 LP: EMI XLP 30019/SXLP 30019

Otello, ballet music

London 16 April 1956	Covent Garden Orchestra	45: HMV 7EP 7069

La traviata

London 18 August- 23 September 1980	English National Opera Orchestra and Chorus Masterson, Brecknock, Du Plessis Sung in English	LP: EMI SLS 5216 CD: EMI CFPSD 4799

Il trovatore, ballet music

London 7 July 1958	Philharmonia	LP: Angel 35751/60354 LP: EMI XLP 30019/SXLP 30019 LP: Quintessence QIMX 7021

I vespri siciliani, ballet music

London 8 January 1958	Philharmonia	LP: Angel 35751/60354 LP: EMI XLP 30019/SXLP 30019 LP: Quintessence QIMX 7021

HENRI VIEUXTEMPS (1820-1881)

Violin Concerto No 5

London 27 April- 18 May 1969	LSO Zukerman	LP: CBS MS 7422/MP 35125/72828 CD: Sony SBK 48276

GIOVANNI VIOTTI (1755-1824)

Violin Concerto No 16, with added parts by Mozart

London 12-14 December 1971	English Chamber Orchestra A.Röhn	LP: DG 2533 122

Violin Concerto No 24

London 12-14 December 1971	English Chamber Orchestra A.Röhn	LP: DG 2533 122

ANTONIO VIVALDI (1678-1741)

Concerto for 2 trumpets and orchestra

London 22-23 May 1976	English Chamber Orchestra André	LP: DG 2530 792/410 8321 CD: DG 415 9802 <u>André plays both solo parts</u>

JAN VORISEK (1791-1825)

Symphony in D

Wembley 19-20 May 1969	English Chamber Orchestra	LP: Philips 6500 203/6527 129
Glasgow 1995	Scottish CO	CD: Hyperion CDA 66880

RICHARD WAGNER (1813-1883)

Götterdämmerung, excerpt (Zu neuen Taten)

Barking Spring 1972	LPO Hunter, Remedios	LP: EMI CFP 40008/CFP 4403 CD: Royal RO 701.902

Götterdämmerung, excerpt (Starke Scheite schichtet mir dort)

Barking Spring 1972	LPO Hunter	LP: EMI CFP 40008/CFP 4403 CD: Royal RO 701.902

Götterdämmerung, Siegfried's Rhine Journey and Funeral march

Barking Spring 1972	LPO	LP: EMI CFP 40008/CFP 4403

Lohengrin, Act 3 prelude

Barking 4-15 June 1970	LPO	LP: EMI CFP 101/CFP 41 10363

Die Meistersinger von Nürnberg

Sydney 14 October 1988	Elizabethan PO Australian Opera Chorus Doese, Gunn, Frey, Pringle, Doig, McIntyre	VHS Video: Polygram 079 2293

Rienzi, overture

London 10 August 1974	BBC SO	CD: Radio Classics BBCRD 9101

WILLIAM WALTON (1902-1983)

Symphony No 1

Watford 9-10 January 1989	LPO	CD: EMI CDEMX 2206

Symphony No 2

Watford 9-10 January 1989	LSO	CD: EMI CDEMX 2206

Siesta for small orchestra

London 28 March 1982	English Chamber Orchestra	CD: Radio Classics 15656 91612
Watford 9-10 January 1989	LSO	EMI unpublished

Henry V, Passacaglia & Touch her sweet lips arranged by Mathieson

London 28 March 1982	English Chamber Orchestra	CD: Radio Classics 15656 91612

PETER WARLOCK (1894-1930)

Capriol suite

London	Sadlers Wells	Columbia unpublished
11 July	Orchestra	
1951		

CARL MARIA VON WEBER (1786-1826)

Piano Concerto No 1

Edinburgh 16-17 April 1994	Scottish CO Demidenko	CD: Hyperion CDA 66729

Piano Concerto No 2

Edinburgh 16-17 April 1994	Scottish CO Demidenko	CD: Hyperion CDA 66729

Konzertstück for piano and orchestra

Walthamstow 18-24 July 1959	Pro Arte Orchestra Cooper	LP: Pye CML 33006
Edinburgh 16-17 April 1994	Scottish CO Demidenko	CD: Hyperion CDA 66729

Aufforderung zum Tanz, arranged by Berlioz

Walthamstow July 1961	LSO	LP: Philips 6539 043 LP: Philips (USA) PHM 500.022/ PHS 900.022 CD: Mercury 434 3522

Abu Hassan, overture

Walthamstow 23 July 1961	LSO	LP: Philips GL 5698 LP: Philips (USA) PHM 500.022/ PHS 900.022 CD: Mercury 434 3522

HENRYK WIENIAWSKI (1835-1880)

Concert polonaise for violin and orchestra

London 27 April- 18 May 1969	LSO Zukerman	LP: CBS MS 7422/72828

DAG WIREN (1905-1986)

Scherzo and March (Serenade for strings)

London 25 October- 30 November 1956	Philharmonia	HMV unpublished

ERMANNO WOLF-FERRARI (1876-1948)

Danza napolitana

London 23-24 October 1956	Philharmonia	45: HMV 7EP 7120 LP: HMV DLP 1193

Festa popolare

London 23-24 October 1956	Philharmonia	LP: HMV DLP 1193

I gioielli della madonna, Act 2 intermezzo

London 23-24 October 1956	Philharmonia	LP: HMV DLP 1193

I gioielli della madonna, Act 3 intermezzo

London 23-24 October 1956	Philharmonia	45: HMV 7EP 7120 LP: HMV DLP 1193

I quattro rusteghi, prelude

London 22 October 1956	Philharmonia	LP: HMV DLP 1193

I quattro rusteghi, intermezzo

London 22 October 1956	Philharmonia	45: HMV 7EP 7120 LP: HMV DLP 1193

Il segreto di Susanna, overture

London 22 October 1956	Philharmonia	45: HMV 7EP 7120 LP: HMV DLP 1193

TRADITIONAL AND MISCELLANEOUS

A hunting we will go, arranged by Mackerras

London 26-27 April 1964	Pro Arte Orchestra Brannigan	LP: EMI CLP 1789/CSD 1542/ESD 7002/ MFP 1014

Ar hyd y nos

London 16-17 April 1959	Masters Chamber Orchestra Lewis	LP: HMV ALP 1777

The ash grove, arranged by Mackerras

London 26-27 April 1964	Pro Arte Orchestra Hendon School Choir	LP: EMI CLP 1789/CSD 1542/ESD 7002/ MFP 1014

The Bay of Biscay, arranged by Tomlinson

London 26-27 April 1964	Pro Arte Orchestra Hendon School Choir Brannigan	LP: EMI CLP 1789/CSD 1542/ESD 7002/ MFP 1014

The bailiff's daughter, arranged by Tomlinson

London 26-27 April 1964	Pro Arte Orchestra Harwood, Brannigan	LP: EMI CLP 1789/CSD 1542/ESD 7002/ MFP 1014

Bingo

London 16-17 April 1959	Masters Chamber Orchestra Lewis	LP: HMV ALP 1777

The briery bush

London 16-17 April 1959	Masters Chamber Orchestra Lewis	LP: HMV ALP 1777

Buy brown buzzems

London 16-17 April 1959	Masters Chamber Orchestra Lewis	LP: HMV ALP 1777

Charlie is my darling, arranged by Tomlinson

London 26-27 April 1964	Pro Arte Orchestra Harwood, Brannigan	LP: EMI CLP 1789/CSD 1542/ESD 7002/ MFP 1014

Dafydd y garreg wen

London 16-17 April 1959	Masters Chamber Orchestra Lewis	LP: HMV ALP 1777

Doctor Foster, arranged by Hughes

London 11-12 January 1962	Pro Arte Orchestra Brannigan	LP: HMV CLP 1557/CSD 1437

The duck and the kangaroo

London 11-12 January 1962	Pro Arte Orchestra Brannigan	LP: HMV CLP 1557/CSD 1437

Early one morning, arranged by Tomlinson

London 26-27 April 1964	Pro Arte Orchestra Harwood	LP: EMI CLP 1789/CSD 1542/ESD 7002/ MFP 1014

Fine flowers in the valley

London 16-17 April 1959	Masters Chamber Orchestra Lewis	LP: HMV ALP 1777

The first Nowell, arranged by Mackerras

London 25 May- 1 July 1957	Philharmonia Orchestra & Chorus Schwarzkopf	LP: Columbia 33CX 1482 LP: Angel 35530/36750 LP: EMI ASD 3798/100 4531 CD: EMI CDM 763 5742

The foggy foggy dew

London 16-17 April 1959	Masters Chamber Orchestra Lewis	LP: HMV ALP 1777

Grad geal mo chridh

London 16-17 April 1959	Masters Chamber Orchestra Lewis	LP: HMV ALP 1777

The Helston furry dance

London 16-17 April 1959	Masters Chamber Orchestra Lewis	LP: HMV ALP 1777

I saw three ships, arranged by Mackerras

London 25 May- 1 July 1957	Philharmonia Orchestra & Chorus Schwarzkopf	LP: Columbia 33CX 1482 LP: Angel 35530/36750 LP: EMI ASD 3798/100 4531 CD: EMI CDM 763 5742

I will give my love an apple

London 16-17 April 1959	Masters Chamber Orchestra Lewis	LP: HMV ALP 1777

In dulci jubilo, arranged by Mackerras

London 25 May- 1 July 1957	Philhasrmonia Orchestra & Chorus Schwarzkopf	LP: Columbia 33CX 1482 LP: Angel 35530/36750 LP: EMI ASD 3798/100 4531 CD: EMI CDM 763 5742

Jack and Jill, arranged by Mackerras

London 11-12 January 1962	Pro Arte Orchestra Brannigan	LP: HMV CLP 1557/CSD 1437

John Peel, arranged by Tomlinson

London 26-27 April 1964	Pro Arte Orchestra Brannigan	LP: EMI CLP 1789/CSD 1542/ESD 7002/ MFP 1014

The jolly beggars, arranged by Mackerras

London 11-12 January 1962	Pro Arte Orchestra Brannigan	LP: HMV CLP 1557/CSD 1437

King Arthur

London 16-17 April 1959	Masters Chamber Orchestra Lewis	LP: HMV ALP 1777

Leezie Lindsay

London 16-17 April 1959	Masters Chamber Orchestra Lewis	LP: HMV ALP 1777

Little Jack Horner, arranged by Mackerras

London 11-12 January 1962	Pro Arte Orchestra Brannigan	LP: HMV CLP 1557/CSD 1437

Maria auf dem Berge, arranged by Mackerras

London 25 May- 1 July 1957	Philharmonia Orchestra & Chorus Schwarzkopf	LP: Columbia 33CX 1482 LP: Angel 35530/36750 LP: EMI ASD 3798/100 5431 CD: EMI CDM 763 5742

The maypole song

London 16-17 April 1959	Masters Chamber Orchestra Lewis	LP: HMV ALP 1777

The miller of Dee, arranged by Mackerras

London	Pro Arte	LP: EMI CLP 1789/CSD 1542/ESD 7002/
26-27	Orchestra	MFP 1014
April	Brannigan	
1964		

Mo nigheann chruinn donn

London	Masters Chamber	LP: HMV ALP 1777
16-17	Orchestra	
April	Lewis	
1959		

The oak and the ash, arranged by Tomlinson

London	Pro Arte	LP: EMI CLP 1789/CSD 1542/ESD 7002/
26-27	Orchestra	MFP 1014
April	Harwood	
1964		

O come all ye faithful, arranged by Mackerras

London	Philharmonia	LP: Columbia 33CX 1482
25 May-	Orchestra & Chorus	LP: Angel 35530/36750
1 July	Schwarzkopf	LP: EMI ASD 3798/100 4531
1957		CD: EMI CDM 763 5742

O du fröhliche, arranged by Mackerras

London	Philharmonia	LP: Columbia 33CX 1482
25 May-	Orchestra & Chorus	LP: Angel 35530/36750
1 July	Schwarzkopf	LP: EMI ASD 3798/100 4531
1957		CD: EMI CDM 763 5742

O love, it is a killing thing

London	Masters Chamber	LP: HMV ALP 1777
16-17	Orchestra	
April	Lewis	
1959		

O Tannenbaum, arranged by Mackerras

London 25 May- 1 July 1957	Philharmonia Orchestra & Chorus Schwarzkopf	Columbia unpublished

O waly waly

London 16-17 April 1959	Masters Chamber Orchestra Lewis	LP: HMV ALP 1777

She moved thro' the fair

London 16-17 April 1959	Masters Chamber Orchestra Lewis	LP: HMV ALP 1777

Sing a song of sixpence, arranged by Mackerras

London 11-12 January 1962	Pro Arte Orchestra Brannigan	LP: HMV CLP 1557/CSD 1437

The stuttering lovers

London 16-17 April 1959	Masters Chamber Orchestra Lewis	LP: HMV ALP 1777

There's none to soothe

London 16-17 April 1959	Masters Chamber Orchestra Lewis	LP: HMV ALP 1777

The vicar of Bray, arranged by Mackerras

London 26-27 April 1964	Pro Arte Orchestra Brannigan	LP: EMI CLP 1789/CSD 1542/ESD 7002/ MFP 1014

Vom Himmel hoch, arranged by Mackerras

London 25 May- 1 July 1957	Philharmonia Orchestra & Chorus Schwarzkopf	LP: Columbia 33CX 1482 LP: Angel 35530/36750 LP: EMI ASD 3798/100 4531 CD: EMI CDM 763 5742

Ye banks and braes, arranged by Tomlinson

London 26-27 April 1964	Pro Arte Orchestra Harwood	LP: EMI CLP 1789/CSD 1542/ESD 7002/ MFP 1014

Simon Rattle
born 1955

With valuable assistance from David Lampon
and Ken Jagger

Discography compiled
by John Hunt

JOHN ADAMS (Born 1947)

The Chairman dances (Nixon in China)

Birmingham 20 September 1993	CBSO	CD: EMI CDC 555 0512

Harmonielehre

Birmingham 4-9 July 1993	CBSO	CD: EMI CDC 555 0512

Short ride in a fast machine

Birmingham 4-9 July 1993	CBSO	CD: EMI CDC 555 0512/CDZ 568 1542/ CDZ 568 3952/CDZ 767 7552

Tromba lontana

Birmingham 4-9 July 1993	CBSO	CD: EMI CDC 555 0512

MALCOLM ARNOLD (Born 1921)

Guitar Concerto

London 6 June 1991	CBSO members Bream	CD: EMI CDC 754 6612 <u>Excerpts</u> CD: EMI CDZ 568 1542/CDZ 767 7552

<u>The abbreviation CBSO throughout this discography denotes City of Birmingham Symphony Orchestra</u>

Photograph of Sir Simon Rattle by Jim Parsons

BELA BARTOK (1881-1945)

Concerto for orchestra

Birmingham 1-3 October 1992	CBSO	CD: EMI CDC 555 0942

Music for strings, percussion and celesta, extract

Birmingham July-August 1995	CBSO	CD: EMI CDM 566 1362

Piano Concerto No 1

Birmingham 22-24 October 1992	CBSO Donohoe	CD: EMI CDC 754 8712

Piano Concerto No 2

Warwick 4-5 October 1990	CBSO Donohoe	CD: EMI CDC 754 8712

Piano Concerto No 3

Birmingham 22-24 October 1992	CBSO Donohoe	CD: EMI CDC 754 8712

Violin Concerto No 2

Cheltenham 23-24 July 1990	CBSO Chung	CD: EMI CDC 754 2112

Violin Rhapsody No 1

Birmingham 31 May- 1 June 1992	CBSO Chung	CD: EMI CDC 754 2112/CDR 569 8062/ CDR 569 9392

Violin Rhapsody No 2

Birmingham 31 May- 1 June 1992	CBSO Chung	CD: EMI CDC 754 2112/CDR 569 8062/ CDR 569 9392

Concerto for 2 pianos, percussion and orchestra

Warwick 20-21 September 1985	CBSO Labèque sisters, Gualda, Drouet	LP: EMI EL 27 04181 CD: EMI CDC 747 4462

Bluebeard's Castle, extract

Birmingham July- August 1995	CBSO Otter, White	CD: EMI CDM 566 1362

The miraculous mandarin, ballet

Birmingham April 1993	CBSO	CD: EMI CDC 555 0942

LUDWIG VAN BEETHOVEN (1770-1827)

Piano Concerto No 1

Warwick 5 October 1995	CBSO Vogt	CD: EMI CDC 556 1792/CDC 556 2662

Piano Concerto No 1, with cadenzas by Glenn Gould

Warwick 5 October 1995	CBSO Vogt	CD: EMI CDC 556 1792/CDC 556 2662/ CDC 556 3712

Piano Concerto No 2

Warwick 3 October 1995	CBSO Vogt	CD: EMI CDC 556 1792/CDC 556 2662/ CDC 556 3712

ALBAN BERG (1885-1935)

Violin Concerto, extract

Birmingham July- August 1995	CBSO Kremer	CD: EMI CDM 566 1372

Lulu suite

Warwick December 1987- April 1988	CBSO Auger	LP: EMI EL 749 8571 CD: EMI CDC 749 8572

FELIX BERNARD (1897-1944)

Dardanella

Wembley 30 December 1986- 2 January 1987	London Sinfonietta	LP: EMI EL 747 9911 CD: EMI CDC 747 9912

LEONARD BERNSTEIN (1918-1990)

Prelude, Fugue and Riffs

Wembley 30 December 1986- 2 January 1987	London Sinfonietta Donohoe, Collins	LP: EMI EL 747 9911 CD: EMI CDC 747 9912/CDZ 252 3342/ CDZ 762 8032/CDC 555 5052

Symphonic dances from West Side Story

Birmingham July-August 1995	CBSO	CD: EMI CDM 566 1372

PIERRE BOULEZ (Born 1925)

Rituel in memoriam Bruno Maderna

Birmingham July-August 1995	CBSO	CD: EMI CDM 566 1362

Columbia Artists' Management
in association with the South Bank Centre
presents

VIENNA PHILHARMONIC ORCHESTRA

SIR SIMON RATTLE
conductor

HAYDN
Symphony No 70 in D

RICHARD STRAUSS
Metamorphosen

BERLIOZ
Symphonie Fantastique

**WEDNESDAY
23 APRIL 1997
AT 7.30PM**

Concert sponsored by Chelsfield plc

Royal Festival Hall RFH ❶

PROGRAMME: £2.00

THE RELUCTANT REVOLUTIONARY
Arnold Schoenberg: His Works and His World

Saturday 28 / Sunday 29 January 1989 at 7.00pm
Royal Festival Hall

City of Birmingham Symphony Orchestra

Simon Rattle conductor

Sharon Sweet Tove
Alfreda Hodgson Waldtaube
John Mitchinson Waldemar
John Rawnsley Bauer
Ian Caley Klaus-Narr
Hans Hotter sprecher
London Symphony Chorus
Richard Hickox Singers

Schoenberg: Gurrelieder (1900-1911)
There will be an interval of 20 minutes between Parts 1 & 2

JOHANNES BRAHMS (1833-1897)

Piano Quartet in G minor, arranged by Schoenberg

Snape	CBSO	LP: EMI EL 27 01691
19 June		CD: EMI CDS 747 3018/CHS 565 5902
1984		Excerpts
		CD: EMI CDZ 252 3342/CDZ 762 8032

BENJAMIN BRITTEN (1913-1976)

War Requiem

Birmingham 27 February- 4 March 1983	CBSO CBSO Chorus Christ Church Boys Choir Söderström, Tear, Allen	LP: EMI SLS 10 77573 CD: EMI CDS 747 0348 Excerpts CD: EMI CDZ 252 3342/CDZ 568 1542/ CDZ 762 8032/CDZ 767 7552

Sinfonia da Requiem

Warwick 23-24 May 1984	CBSO	LP: EMI EL 27 02631 CD: EMI CDC 555 3942/CDS 754 2702/ CDM 764 8702

Diversions for piano and orchestra

Warwick 15-17 July 1990	CBSO Donohoe	CD: EMI CDS 754 2702

Variations and Fugue on a theme of Purcell

Birmingham 28 January 1995	CBSO	CD: EMI CDC 555 3942
Birmingham 2 June 1995	CBSO	CD-Rom: EMI CDRM 491 6162 <u>CD-Rom also includes a spoken commentary</u> <u>by Rattle and an additional variation on</u> <u>the Purcell theme composed by Judith Weir;</u> <u>CD-Rom package also contains a copy of</u> <u>the separate CD</u>

American overture

Warwick 23-24 May 1984	CBSO	LP: EMI EL 27 02631 CD: EMI CDC 555 3942/CDS 754 2702/ CDM 764 8702

Occasional overture

Warwick 23-24 May 1984	CBSO	LP: EMI EL 27 02631 CD: EMI CDM 754 2702

Building of the House overture

Warwick 15-17 July 1990	CBSO	CD: EMI CDS 754 2702

Canadian Carnival

Cheltenham 22-23 April 1982	CBSO	LP: EMI ASD 4177 CD: EMI CDS 754 2702

Scottish Ballad for 2 pianos and orchestra

Cheltenham 22-23 April 1982	CBSO Donohoe, Fowke	LP: EMI ASD 4177 CD: EMI CDS 754 2702

A time there was, suite

Warwick 23-24 May 1984	CBSO	LP: EMI EL 27 02631 CD: EMI CDC 555 3942/CDS 754 2702

Young Apollo

Cheltenham 22-23 April 1982	CBSO	LP: EMI ASD 4177 CD: EMI CDS 754 2702

Russian Funeral march

Birmingham December 1994	CBSO	CD: EMI CDC 555 4762

Ballad of Heroes, cantata

Warwick 15-17 July 1990	CBSO CBSO Chorus Tear	CD: EMI CDS 754 2702

Praise we great men, fragment completed by Matthews

Warwick 15-17 July 1990	CBSO CBSO Chorus Hargan, M.King, Tear, White	CD: EMI CDS 754 2702

4 chansons françaises

Cheltenham 22-23 April 1982	CBSO Gomez	LP: EMI ASD 4177 CD: EMI CDS 754 2702

ANTON BRUCKNER (1824-1896)

Symphony No 7

Birmingham 17-18 September 1996	CBSO	CD: EMI CDC 556 4252

ELLIOTT CARTER (Born 1908)

A celebration of some 100 x 150 notes

Birmingham 7 August 1995	CBSO	CD: EMI CDM 566 1372

HENRY CREAMER (1879-1930)

After you've gone

Wembley 30 December 1986- 2 January 1987	London Sinfonietta J.Taylor	LP: EMI EL 747 9911 CD: EMI CDC 747 9912

CLAUDE DEBUSSY (1862-1918)

Images pour orchestre

Warwick February 1989	CBSO	LP: EMI EL 749 9471 CD: EMI CDC 749 9472/CDR 572 0952/ CDR 572 0962 <u>Excerpts</u> CD: EMI CDZ 568 1542/CDZ 767 7552

Jeux

Warwick February 1989	CBSO	LP: EMI EL 749 9471 CD: EMI CDC 749 9472/CDR 572 0952/ CDR 572 0962 <u>Excerpts</u> CD: EMI CDM 566 1372

Pagodes, arranged by Grainger

Birmingham December 1996	CBSO	CD: EMI CDC 556 4122

2 movements from King Lear, arranged by Roger-Ducasse

Warwick February 1989	CBSO	LP: EMI EL 749 9471 CD: EMI CDC 749 9472/CDR 572 0952/ CDR 572 0962

WALTER DONALDSON (1893-1947)

Makin' Whoopee!; My blue heaven

Wembley	London	LP: EMI EL 747 9911
30 December	Sinfonietta	CD: EMI CDC 747 9912
1986-	Harvey and the	
2 January	Wallbangers	
1987		

PATRICK DOYLE (Born 1953)

Henry V, incidental music

Wembley	CBSO	LP: EMI EL 749 9191
March		CD: EMI CDC 749 9192
1989		<u>Film soundtrack</u>
		<u>Excerpts</u>
		CD: EMI CDZ 568 3952

EDWARD ELGAR (1857-1934)

The Dream of Gerontius

Warwick 6-8 September 1986	CBSO CBSO Chorus Baker, Mitchinson, Shirley-Quirk	LP: EMI EX 749 5491 CD: EMI CDS 749 5492 <u>Excerpts</u> CD: EMI CDZ 252 3342/CDZ 568 1542/ CDZ 762 8032/CDZ 767 7552

Violin Concerto

Birmingham July 1997	CBSO Kennedy	CD: EMI CDC 556 4132

Enigma Variations

Birmingham 28-29 August 1993	CBSO	CD: EMI CDC 555 0012

Falstaff

Warwick 24-25 April 1992	CBSO	CD: EMI CDC 555 0012

Grania and Diarmid, incidental music and funeral march

Birmingham 28-29 August 1993	CBSO	CD: EMI CDC 555 0012

MANUEL DE FALLA (1876-1946)

El retable de Maese Pedro

London 17-19 April 1979	London Sinfonietta J.Smith, Oliver, Knapp	LP: Decca ZRG 921 CD: Decca 433 9082

Harpsichord Concerto

London 17-19 April 1979	London Sinfonietta Constable	LP: Decca ZRG 921 CD: Decca 433 9082

Psyché

London 17-19 April 1979	London Sinfonietta J.Smith	LP: Decca ZRG 921 CD: Decca 433 9082

GEORGE GERSHWIN (1898-1937)

Porgy and Bess

London
8-19
February
1988
	LPO
	Glyndebourne
	Festival Chorus
	Haymon, Clarey,
	Blackwell,
	D.Evans, White
		LP: EMI EX 749 5681
		CD: EMI CDS 749 5682/CDS 556 2202
		VHS Video: EMI MVB 491 1313
		Laserdisc: EMI LDD 491 1311
		Excerpts
		CD: EMI CDC 754 3252/CDH 565 0722/
		    CDZ 252 3342/CDZ 568 1542/
		    CDZ 568 3952/CDZ 762 8032/
		    CDZ 767 7552/CDC 555 5052
		Filming sessions, for which the original
		soundtrack was used, took place between
		21 November and 18 December 1992

Piano Concerto

Warwick 4-6 October 1990	CBSO Donohoe	CD: EMI CDC 754 2802/CDM 764 3042/ CDM 764 3052

Rhapsody in Blue

Wembley 30 December 1986- 2 January 1987	London Sinfonietta Donohoe	LP: EMI EL 747 9911 CD: EMI CDC 747 9912/CDC 754 2802

Rhapsody in Blue, extract

Birmingham July-August 1995	CBSO Marshall	CD: EMI CDM 566 1372

BERTHOLD GOLDSCHMIDT (1903-1996)

Ciaccona sinfonica

Birmingham   CBSO   CD: Decca 452 5992
July
1995

Passacaglia

Birmingham   CBSO   CD: Decca 452 5992
July
1995

PERCY GRAINGER (1882-1961)

In a nutshell

Birmingham   CBSO   CD: EMI CDC 556 4122
December
1996

Train music, arranged by Rathburn

Birmingham   CBSO   CD: EMI CDC 556 4122
December
1996

The warriors, music to an imaginary ballet

Birmingham   CBSO   CD: EMI CDC 556 4122
December
1996

A Lincolnshire posy

Birmingham   CBSO   CD: EMI CDC 556 4122
December
1996

A country garden

Birmingham   CBSO   CD: EMI CDC 556 4122
December
1996

EDVARD GRIEG (1843-1907)

Piano Concerto

Warwick 21-24 April 1992	CBSO Vogt	CD: EMI CDC 754 7462 <u>Excerpts</u> CD: EMI CDZ 568 3952/CDR 572 1112/ CDR 572 1122

SOFIA GUBAIDULINA (Born 1931)

Zeitgestalten, extract

Birmingham July-August 1995	CBSO	CD: EMI CDM 566 1372

FRANZ JOSEF HAYDN (1732-1809)

Die Schöpfung

Warwick 24 March- 29 April 1990	CBSO CBSO Chorus Auger, Langridge, D.Thomas Sung in English	CD: EMI CDS 754 1592 Excerpts CD: EMI CDZ 568 1542/CDZ 767 7552

Symphony No 22 "Philosopher"

Birmingham 2 December 1994	CBSO	CD: EMI CDC 555 5092

Symphony No 60 "Il distratto"

Warwick 26 October- 22 December 1990	CBSO	CD: EMI CDC 754 2972 Excerpts CD: EMI CDZ 568 3952/CDZ 568 1542/ CDZ 767 7552

Symphony No 70

Warwick 26 October- 22 December 1990	CBSO	CD: EMI CDC 754 2972

Symphony No 86

Birmingham 30-31 July 1994	CBSO	CD: EMI CDC 555 5092

Symphony No 90

Warwick 26 October- 22 December 1990	CBSO	CD: EMI CDC 754 2972

Symphony No 102

Birmingham 7-8 October 1994	CBSO	CD: EMI CDC 555 5092

HANS WERNER HENZE (Born 1926)

Symphony No 7

Birmingham	CBSO	CD: EMI CDC 754 7622
25 May		Excerpt
1992		CD: EMI CDZ 568 3952

Symphony No 8, extract

Birmingham	CBSO	CD: EMI CDM 566 1372
July-August		
1995		

Barcarola per grande orchestra

Birmingham	CBSO	CD: EMI CDC 754 7622
25 May		
1992		

GUSTAV HOLST (1874-1934)

The Planets

London	Philharmonia	LP: EMI ASD 4047
29-30	Ambrosian	CD: EMI CDM 764 7402/CDB 572 1392
December	Singers	
1980		

CHARLES IVES (1874-1954)

Decoration Day, extract

Birmingham	CBSO	CD: EMI CDM 566 1372
July-August		
1995		

LEOS JANACEK (1854-1928)

The cunning little vixen

London 9-17 June 1990	Covent Garden Orchestra & Chorus Watson, Montague, Tear, Allen, Howell, Folwell Sung in English	CD: EMI CDS 754 2122 Excerpts CD: EMI CDZ 568 1542/CDZ 767 7552

Glagolithic Mass

Birmingham 9-10 January 1981	CBSO CBSO Chorus Palmer, Gunson, Mitchinson, M.King	LP: EMI ASD 4066/2C 069 07597 CD: EMI CDC 747 5042 Excerpts CD: EMI CDZ 568 1542/CDZ 767 7552

Sinfonietta

London 17-18 November 1982	Philharmonia	LP: EMI ASD 143 5221 CD: EMI CDC 747 0482/CDC 747 5042 CDM 764 7402 Excerpts CD: EMI CDZ 252 3342/CDZ 762 8032

Taras Bulba

London 17-18 November 1982	Philharmonia	LP: EMI ASD 143 5221 CD: EMI CDC 747 0482/CDS 754 2122

GUS KAHN (1886-1941)

Nobody's sweetheart

Wembley 30 December 1986- 2 January 1987	London Sinfonietta	LP: EMI EL 747 9911 CD: EMI CDC 747 9912

OLIVER KNUSSEN (Born 1952)

Flourish with fireworks

Birmingham 7 August 1995	CBSO	CD: EMI CDM 566 1372

e Orchestra of the Age of Enlightenment

6.30 pm
Wednesday
29 November 1995
at the
Royal Festival Hall
RFH ❶

W.A. Mozart

Così fan tutte
Concert Performance

SIR SIMON RATTLE
conductor

KURT STREIT
Ferrando

GERALD FINLEY
Guglielmo

THOMAS ALLEN
Don Alfonso

HILLEVI MARTINPELTO
Fiordiligi

ALISON HAGLEY
Dorabella

ANN MURRAY
Despina

The CHOIR of the ENLIGHTENMENT

Sponsored by
PHOENIX GROUP LIMITED

GLYNDEBOURNE FESTIVAL OPERA

with

THE LONDON PHILHARMONIC ORCHESTRA

Concert performance

IDOMENEO

Opera in three acts by W. A. Mozart
Text by Abbate Varesco
Published by Bärenreiter Verlag, Kassel

Sung in the original Italian

Conductor Simon Rattle

Cast (in order of singing)

Ilia, *a Trojan princess, daughter of Priam*	Yvonne Kenny
Idamante, *Prince of Crete, son of Idomeneo*	John Aler
Electra, *daughter of Agamemnon*	Elizabeth Connell
Arbace, *counsellor to Idomeneo*	David Johnston
Idomeneo, *King of Crete*	Philip Langridge
High Priest	Anthony Roden
Voice of Neptune	Geoffrey Moses
Harpsichord continuo played by	Jonathan Hinden
Cello continuo played by	Mark Jackson

The opera was first performed in Munich, 29 January 1781 and first performed at Glyndebourne 20 June 1951 (first professional stage performance in England).

The performance being given this evening is a concert version of the production, directed by Trevor Nunn, first given at Glyndebourne in May 1983 and revived for the 1985 Glyndebourne Festival. Trevor Nunn is Joint Artistic Director of the Royal Shakespeare Company

The production was sponsored by Intobarp Group Limited

Curtain up 6.30 p. m.   Supper Interval 8.20 p. m.   Curtain down 10.20 p. m. approximately

The audience is particularly asked to refrain from applauding until the end of a scene or aria
The taking of photographs and the use of recording equipment in the auditorium are forbidden.

FRANZ LISZT (1811-1886)

A Faust symphony

Berlin 15-17 April 1994	BPO Senff and Prague Choirs Seiffert	CD: EMI CDC 555 2202

Piano Concerto No 1

Warwick 25-26 March 1982	CBSO Ousset	LP: EMI ASD 4307 CD: EMI CDC 747 2212

WITOLD LUTOSLAWSKI (1913-1994)

Symphony No 3, extract

Birmingham July-August 1995	CBSO	CD: EMI CDM 566 1362

Jeux vénitiens, extract

Birmingham July-August 1995	CBSO	CD: EMI CDM 566 1362

GUSTAV MAHLER (1860-1911)

Symphony No 1 "Titan"

Birmingham 16-17 December 1991	CBSO	CD: EMI CDC 754 6472 <u>Contains Blumine movement</u> <u>Excerpts</u> CD: EMI CDZ 568 1542/CDZ 568 3952/ CDZ 767 7552

Symphony No 2 "Resurrection"

Watford 27 April- 1 June 1986	CBSO CBSO Chorus Auger, Baker	LP: EMI EL 27 05983 CD: EMI CDS 747 9628 <u>Excerpts</u> CD: EMI CDZ 252 3342/CDZ 568 1542/ CDZ 762 8032/CDZ 767 7552

Symphony No 4

Birmingham 8-9 May 1997	CBSO Roocroft	CD: EMI awaiting publication

Symphony No 6

Watford 14-16 December 1989	CBSO	LP: EMI EX 754 0491 CD: EMI CDS 754 0472 <u>Excerpts</u> CD: EMI CDZ 568 1542/CDZ 767 7552

Symphony No 7

Snape 21-22 June 1991	CBSO	CD: EMI CDC 754 3442 <u>Excerpts</u> CD: EMI CDZ 767 1542/CDZ 767 7552/ CDM 566 1372

<u>The published version of this symphony is a live concert performance: a previous studio recording remains unpublished</u>

Symphony No 9

Vienna 4-5 December 1993	VPO	CD: EMI awaiting publication

Symphony No 10, arranged by Cooke

Southampton 10-12 June 1980	Bournemouth SO	LP: EMI SLS 5206 CD: EMI CDS 747 3018/CDC 754 4062

Das Lied von der Erde

Warwick 28-30 December 1995	CBSO Seiffert, Hampson	CD: EMI CDC 556 2002

Das Lied von der Erde, extract

Birmingham July-August 1995	CBSO Otter	CD: EMI CDM 566 1362

Das klagende Lied

Birmingham 12-13 October 1983- 24 June 1984	CBSO CBSO Chorus Doese, Hodgson, Tear, Rea	LP: EMI EL 27 01361 CD: EMI CDC 747 0892

NICHOLAS MAW (Born 1935)

Odyssey

Birmingham 11 October 1990	CBSO	CD: EMI CDS 754 2772 <u>Excerpts</u> CD: EMI CDZ 568 1542/CDZ 767 7552

PETER MAXWELL DAVIES (Born 1934)

Symphony No 1

London 10-15 August 1978	Philharmonia	LP: Decca HEAD 21

LINDSAY MCPHAIL (1895-1965)

San

Wembley 30 December 1986- 2 January 1987	London Sinfonietta	LP: EMI EL 747 9911 CD: EMI CDC 747 9912/CDZ 568 1542/ CDZ 767 7552

OLIVIER MESSIAEN (1908-1992)

Turangalîla Symphony

Warwick
30 January-
1 February
1986
	CBSO
	Donohoe, Murail
		LP: EMI EX 27 04683
		CD: EMI CDS 747 4638
		Excerpts
		CD: EMI CDZ 252 3342/CDZ 568 1542/
		    CDZ 762 8032/CDZ 767 7552/
		    CDM 566 1362

Et expecto resurrectionem mortuorum, extract

Birmingham 7 August 1995	CBSO	CD: EMI CDM 566 1372

DARIUS MILHAUD (1892-1974)

La création du monde

Wembley 30 December 1986- 2 January 1987	London Sinfonietta Harle	LP: EMI EL 747 9911 CD: EMI CDC 747 9912

WOLFGANG AMADEUS MOZART (1756-1791)

Così fan tutte

Birmingham 1-3 December 1995	Age of Enlightenment Orchestra & Chorus Martinpelto, Hagley, Murray, Streit, Finley, Allen	CD: EMI CDS 556 1702 Includes supplementary arias

CARL NIELSEN (1865-1931)

Symphony No 4 "Inextinguishable"

Warwick 13-14 September 1984	CBSO	LP: EMI EL 27 02601 CD: EMI CDC 747 5032/CDM 764 7372

Pan and Syrinx

Warwick 13-14 September 1984	CBSO	LP: EMI EL 27 02601 CD: EMI CDC 747 5032/CDM 764 7372 Excerpts CD: EMI CDZ 252 3342/CDZ 762 8032

SERGEI PROKOFIEV (1891-1953)

Symphony No 5

Birmingham 24-26 January 1992	CBSO	CD: EMI CDC 754 5772 Excerpt CD: EMI CDZ 568 3952

Piano Concerto No 1

London 7-9 July 1977	LSO Gavrilov	LP: EMI ASD 3571/EG 29 03261 CD: EMI CDM 764 3292/CDM 769 0262

Scythian suite

Birmingham 24-26 January 1992	CBSO	CD: EMI CDC 754 5772

SERGEI RACHMANINOV (1873-1943)

Symphony No 2

Los Angeles 2-3 January 1984	Los Angeles PO	LP: EMI EL 27 00521 CD: EMI CDC 747 0622

Piano Concerto No 2

Birmingham 24-25 June 1983	CBSO Ousset	EMI unpublished
Warwick 3-4 May 1984	CBSO Ousset	LP: EMI EL 27 01031 CD: EMI CDC 747 2232/CDD 763 9032/ CDB 572 1422

Rhapsody on a theme of Paganini

Birmingham 24-25 June 1983	CBSO Ousset	EMI unpublished
Warwick 3-4 May 1984	CBSO Ousset	LP: EMI EL 27 01031 CD: EMI CDC 747 2232/CDM 764 4402/ CDB 572 1422

Symphonic dances

Snape 23 October 1982	CBSO	LP: EMI ASD 143 6111

Vocalise

Birmingham 28 February 1983	CBSO	LP: EMI ASD 143 6111 CD: EMI CHS 565 5902

MAURICE RAVEL (1875-1937)

Piano Concerto in G

Warwick 26-27 April 1990	CBSO Ousset	CD: EMI CDC 754 1582

Piano Concerto for the left hand

London 7-9 July 1977	LSO Gavrilov	LP: EMI ASD 3571/EG 29 03251 CD: EMI CDM 769 0262
Warwick 26-27 April 1990	CBSO Ousset	CD: EMI CDC 754 1582

Alborada del gracioso

Warwick October 1989	CBSO	CD: EMI CDC 754 2042

Boléro

Warwick 16-21 December 1990	CBSO	CD: EMI CDC 754 3032/CDR 569 8302/ CDR 569 9632

Chansons madécasses

London 25 May 1975	Nash Ensemble Palmer	LP: Decca ZRG 834 <u>Rattle's first recording sessions</u>

Daphnis et Chloé

Warwick 16-21 December 1990	CBSO CBSO Chorus	CD: EMI CDC 754 3032/CDR 569 8032/ CDR 569 9632

Fanfare pour l'éventail de Jeanne

Warwick October 1989	CBSO	CD: EMI CDC 754 2042

Ma mère l'oye

Warwick April 1990	CBSO	CD: EMI CDC 754 2042

3 poèmes de Mallarmé

London	Nash Ensemble	LP: Decca ZRG 834
25 May	Palmer	Rattle's first recording sessions
1975		

Shéhérazade

Warwick	CBSO	CD: EMI CDC 754 2042
October	Ewing	Excerpts
1989		CD: EMI CDZ 568 1542/CDZ 767 7552

La vallée des cloches, arranged by Grainger

Warwick	CBSO	CD: EMI CDC 754 2042/CDC 556 4122
April		
1990		

La valse

Warwick	CBSO	CD: EMI CDC 754 2042
April		
1990		

JOAQUIN RODRIGO (Born 1901)

Guitar Concerto

Warwick 28 October 1990	CBSO Bream	CD: EMI CDC 754 6612

CAMILLE SAINT-SAENS (1835-1921)

Piano Concerto No 2

Warwick 25-26 March 1982	CBSO Ousset	LP: EMI ASD 4307 CD: EMI CDC 747 2212/CDB 572 1512

ARNOLD SCHOENBERG (1874-1951)

Orchestral variations

| Birmingham
5-6
April
1993 | CBSO | CD: EMI CDC 555 2122 |

5 Orchestral pieces

| Warwick
December
1987-
April
1988 | CBSO | LP: EMI EL 749 8571
CD: EMI CDC 749 8572
Excerpts
CD: EMI CDZ 568 1542/CDZ 767 7552 |

Chamber Symphony No 1

| Birmingham
9-10
October
1993 | Birmingham
Contemporary
Music Group | CD: EMI CDC 555 2122 |

Pierrot lunaire

London 22-23 February 1977	Nash Ensemble Manning	LP: Chandos ABR 1046 CD: Chandos CHAN 6534

Erwartung

Birmingham 30 September– 1 October 1993	CBSO Bryn-Julson	CD: EMI CDC 555 2122

A survivor from Warsaw

Birmingham 7 August 1995	CBSO CBSO Chorus Mazura	CD: EMI CDM 566 1362

ROBERT SCHUMANN (1810-1856)

Piano Concerto

Warwick 22-24 April 1992	CBSO Vogt	CD: EMI CDC 754 7462

DIMITRI SHOSTAKOVICH (1906-1975)

Symphony No 4

Birmingham July 1994	CBSO	CD: EMI CDC 555 4762

Symphony No 10

London 3-4 April 1985	Philharmonia	LP: EMI EL 27 03151 CD: EMI CDC 747 3503/CDM 764 8702 <u>Excerpts</u> CD: EMI CDZ 252 3342/CDZ 762 8032

Symphony No 14, *extract*

Birmingham July-August 1995	CBSO White	CD: EMI CDM 566 1362

JEAN SIBELIUS (1865-1957)

Symphony No 1

Warwick 7-13 December 1984	CBSO	LP: EMI EL 27 03091 CD: EMI CDM 764 1192/CMS 764 1182 <u>Excerpts</u> CD: EMI CDZ 568 1542/CDZ 767 7552

Symphony No 2

Warwick 21-22 June 1984	CBSO	LP: EMI EL 27 01601 CD: EMI CDM 764 1202/CMS 764 1182

Symphony No 3

Warwick 10-11 October 1905	CBSO	LP: EMI EL 27 04961 CD: EMI CDC 747 6202/CDM 764 1202/ CMS 764 1182 <u>Excerpts</u> CD: EMI CDZ 568 1542/CDZ 767 7552

Symphony No 4

Warwick 13-14 December 1986	CBSO	CD: EMI CDC 747 7112/CDM 764 1212/ CMS 764 1182

Symphony No 5

London 9-10 October 1981	Philharmonia	LP: EMI ASD 4168/2C 069 07586 CD: EMI CDC 747 0062/CDM 764 7372

Warwick
21 February
1987
	CBSO	CD: EMI CDC 749 7172/CDM 764 1222/
		    CMS 764 1182
		Excerpts
		CD: EMI CDZ 252 3342/CDZ 568 1542/
		    CDZ 568 3952/CDZ 762 8032/
		    CDZ 767 7552

Symphony No 6

Warwick 13-14 December 1986	CBSO	CD: EMI CDC 747 7112/CDM 764 1212/ CMS 764 1182

Symphony No 7

Warwick 10-11 October 1985	CBSO	LP: EMI EL 27 04961 CD: EMI CDC 747 6202/CDM 764 1222/ CMS 764 1182

Violin Concerto

Warwick 8-9 February 1987	CBSO Kennedy	CD: EMI CDC 749 7172/CDC 754 1272/ CDC 754 5592

 WEDNESDAY 8 MARCH

Conductor: **Sir Simon Rattle**
Soloist: **Felicity Lott**

City of Birmingham Symphony Orchestra

Leader: Peter Thomas

Appalachian Spring	**Copland**
Closing Scene from *Capriccio*, **Op 85**	**Strauss**

INTERVAL

Symphony No 5 in D	**Vaughan Williams**

Tonight's performance is being broadcast live on BBC Radio 3.

Sponsored by

The CBSO Society Ltd gratefully acknowledges the support of Midland Bank, sponsor of tonight's concert.

CBSO Society Limited
Paradise Place
Birmingham
B3 3RP
Tel: 0121 236 1555
Fax: 0121 233 2423

Patron:
HRH The Prince Edward CVO
Chief Executive:
Edward Smith

The CBSO receives financial assistance from the Arts Council of England and Birmingham City Council.

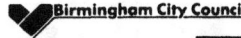

THURSDAY 13 APRIL

Conductor:
Sir Simon Rattle
Soloist: **Gundula Janowitz**

City of Birmingham Symphony Orchestra

Co-Leader: Lyn Fletcher

Symphony No 33 in B flat, K319	Mozart
Five Songs with Orchestra	Strauss
Ruhe, meine Seele! Op 27, No 1	
Waldseligkeit, Op 49, No 1	
Morgen! Op 27, No 4	
Wiegenlied, Op 41, No 1	
Befreit, Op 39, No 4	

INTERVAL

Symphony No 3 in D major, D200	Schubert
Parsifal: Good Friday Music	Wagner

Sponsored by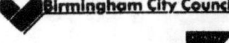
The CBSO Society Ltd gratefully acknowledges the support of
British Airways, sponsor of tonight's concert.

CBSO Society Limited
Paradise Place
Birmingham
B3 3RP
Tel: 0121 236 1555
Fax: 0121 233 2423

Patron:
HRH The Prince Edward CVO
Chief Executive:
Edward Smith

The CBSO receives financial assistance from the Arts Council of England and Birmingham City Council.

Birmingham City Council

THE ARTS COUNCIL OF ENGLAND

Night ride and sunrise

London 9-10 October 1981	Philharmonia	LP: EMI ASD 4168/2C 069 07586 CD: EMI CDC 747 0062/CMS 764 1182/ CDM 764 1222

The Oceanides

Warwick 7-13 December 1984	CBSO	LP: EMI EL 27 03091 CD: EMI CDM 764 1192/CMS 764 1182

Scene with cranes (Kuolema)

Warwick 4 May 1984	CBSO	LP: EMI EL 27 01601 CD: EMI CDM 764 1222/CMS 764 1182

RICHARD STRAUSS (1864-1949)

Metamorphosen

Vienna 19-20 April 1997	VPO	CD: EMI awaiting publication

Elektra, excerpt (Denn du bist klug)

Birmingham July-August 1995	CBSO Palmer	CD: EMI CDM 566 1372

4 letzte Lieder

Birmingham July-August 1995	CBSO Roocroft	CD: EMI awaiting publication <u>Im Abendrot</u> CD: EMI CDM 566 1362

IGOR STRAVINSKY (1882-1971)

Symphony in 3 movements

Warwick 3-4 October 1986	CBSO	LP: EMI EL 749 0531 CD: EMI CDC 749 0532

Suites 1 and 2

Newcastle- upon-Tyne 29 March 1977- 3 January 1978	Northern Sinfonia	LP: EMI ASD 3604 CD: EMI CDM 764 7392/CDM 769 2042

Le sacre du printemps

London 14-15 April 1977	National Youth Orchestra	LP: Enigma MID 5001 LP: ASV ACM 2030 CD: ASV CDQS 6031
Warwick December 1987	CBSO	LP: EMI EL 749 6361 CD: EMI CDC 749 6362 <u>Excerpts</u> CD: EMI CDZ 568 1542/CDZ 767 7552

Le sacre du printemps, extract

Birmingham July-August 1995	CBSO	CD: EMI CDM 566 1362

Agon, extract

Birmingham July-August 1995	CBSO	CD: EMI CDM 566 1362

Apollon musagète

Warwick April 1988	CBSO	LP: EMI EL 749 6361 CD: EMI CDC 749 6362

Ebony Concerto

Wembley 30 December 1986- 2 January 1987	London Sinfonietta Collins	LP: EMI EL 747 9911 CD: EMI CDC 747 9912

4 études

Warwick October 1987	CBSO	CD: EMI CDC 749 1782

3 Japanese lyrics

London 13-14 February 1977	Nash Ensemble Manning	LP: Chandos ABR 1048 CD: Chandos CHAN 6535

L'oiseau de feu, ballet

Warwick October 1987	CBSO	CD: EMI CDC 749 1782 Excerpts CD: EMI CDZ 252 3342/CDZ 762 8032

Petrushka, 1947 version

Warwick 3-4 October 1986	CBSO Donohoe	LP: EMI EL 749 0531 CD: EMI CDC 749 0532 Excerpts CD: EMI CDZ 568 1542/CDZ 767 7552

Pulcinella

Newcastle- upon-Tyne 28-29 March 1977- 3-4 January 1978	Northern Sinfonia J.Smith, Fryatt, King	LP: EMI ASD 3604 CD: EMI CDM 764 7392

Ragtime for 11 instruments

Birmingham October 1989	CBSO members	CD: EMI CDZ 568 1542/CDZ 568 3952/ CDZ 767 7552

Scherzo à la russe, orchestral version

Warwick October 1987	CBSO	CD: EMI CDC 749 1782

Scherzo à la russe, jazz version

Warwick October 1987	CBSO members	CD: EMI CDC 749 1782

Symphonies of wind instruments

London 13-14 February 1977	Nash Ensemble	LP: Chandos ABR 1048 CD: Chandos CHAN 6535

KAROL SZYMANOWSKI (1882-1937)

Symphony No 3

Birmingham 1-2 October 1993	CBSO CBSO Chorus Garrison	CD: EMI CDC 555 1212

Violin Concerto No 1

Birmingham April 1995	CBSO Zehetmair	CD: EMI CDC 555 6072

Violin Concerto No 2

Birmingham April 1995	CBSO Zehetmair	CD: EMI CDC 555 6072

Stabat mater

Birmingham 3-4 April 1993	CBSO CBSO Chorus Szmytka Quivar, J.Connell	CD: EMI CDC 555 1212 Excerpts <u>CD</u>: EMI CDZ 568 1542/CDZ 568 3952/ CDZ 767 7552

Litania do Marii Panny

Birmingham April 1993	CBSO CBSO Chorus Szmytka	CD: EMI CDC 555 1212

254 Rattle

TORU TAKEMITSU (1930-1996)

To the edge of dream, for guitar and orchestra

Warwick 28 February 1992	CBSO Bream	CD: EMI CDC 754 6612

Dream/Window, extract

Birmingham July-August 1995	CBSO	CD: EMI CDC 566 1372

MARK-ANTHONY TURNAGE (Born 1960)

Drowned out

Birmingham 18 March 1994	CBSO	CD: EMI CDC 555 0912 <u>Excerpt</u> <u>CD: EMI CDM 566 1372</u>

Kai

Birmingham 10 June 1993	Birmingham Contemporary Music Group Heinen	CD: EMI CDC 555 0912

Momentum

Birmingham 29 August 1993	CBSO	CD: EMI CDC 555 0912

3 Screaming Popes

Birmingham 26 January 1992	CBSO	CD: EMI CDC 555 0912 <u>Also issued as a CD single</u>

EDGAR VARESE (1883-1965)

Ionisation, extract

Birmingham July-August 1995	CBSO	CD: EMI CDM 566 1362

RALPH VAUGHAN WILLIAMS (1872-1958)

The lark ascending, for violin and orchestra

Birmingham July 1997	CBSO Kennedy	CD: EMI CDC 556 4132

Songs of travel

Birmingham 16-27 May 1983	CBSO Allen	LP: EMI EL 27 00591 CD: EMI CDC 747 2202/CDM 764 7312

On Wenlock Edge

Birmingham 16-27 May 1983	CBSO Tear	LP: EMI EL 27 00591 CD: EMI CDC 747 2202/CDM 764 7312

WILLIAM WALTON (1902-1983)

Symphony No 1

Warwick 21-22 October 1990	CBSO	CD: EMI CDC 754 5722

Cello Concerto

Warwick 21 December 1991	CBSO Harrell	CD: EMI CDC 754 5722

ANTON VON WEBERN (1883-1945)

6 orchestral pieces

Warwick December 1987- April 1988	CBSO	LP: EMI EL 749 8571 CD: EMI CDC 749 8572

5 orchestral pieces, nos. 3-5

Birmingham July-August 1995	CBSO	CD: EMI CDM 566 1372

Concertino for 9 instruments

London 22-23 February 1977	Nash Ensemble	LP: Chandos ABR 1046 CD: Chandos CHAN 6534

KURT WEILL (1900-1950)

Die 7 Todsünden

Birmingham 7 September 1982	CBSO Ross, Caley, Rolfe-Johnson, Tomlinson	LP: EMI ASD 4402/2C 069 07698 CD: EMI CDM 764 7392

VICTOR YOUNG (1900-1956)

Sweet Sue

Wembley 30 December 1986- 2 January 1987	London Sinfonietta Harvey and the Wallbangers	LP: EMI EL 747 9911 CD: EMI CDC 747 9912

John Pritchard
1921-1989

Discography compiled by John Hunt

BELA BARTOK (1881-1945)

Concerto for orchestra

Barking 20-22 July 1971	LPO	LP: EMI CFP 176/CFP 4504

Piano Concerto No 3

London November 1966	Pro Arte Orchestra Siki	LP: Pye GGC 4054/GSGC 14054

LUDWIG VAN BEETHOVEN (1770-1827)

Symphony No 1

Vienna 28-29 April 1953	Vienna SO	LP: Philips A00179L/G03037L/ GBL 5539/S06037R/G03003L LP: Epic LC 3095

Symphony No 6 "Pastoral"

London 28 August 1975	LSO	Unpublished radio broadcast

Symphony No 7

London 4 October 1985	BBC SO	CD: Radio Classics 15656 91322

Piano Concerto No 2

London 12 August 1972	BBC SO Rosen	Unpublished radio broadcast

Violin Concerto

London 10-12 August 1961	RPO Campoli	LP: EMI XLP 20043/SXLP 20043/CFP 40299

Triple Concerto

London 21 January 1970	BBC SO Roll, I.Brown, Igloi	Unpublished radio broadcast

Violin Romance No 1

London 20 November- 16 December 1960	Philharmonia Menuhin	LP: HMV ALP 2070/ASD 618/SXLP 30249 CD: EMI CDM 764 3242

Violin Romance No 2

London 20 November- March 1965	Philharmonia Menuhin	LP: HMV ALP 2070/ASD 618/SXLP 30249 CD: EMI CDM 764 3242

Mass in C

London 22 July 1983	BBC SO BBC Choirs LPO Choir Cotrubas, Kuhlmann, Tear, Howell	CD: Radio Classics 15656 91552

Choral Fantasy

London 6 October 1985	BBC SO BBC Singers Vogel	CD: Radio Classics 15656 91322

Leonore No 1, overture

London 6 October 1985	BBC SO	CD: Radio Classics 15656 91322

VINCENZO BELLINI (1801-1835)

I Capuleti ed i Montecchi

London 21 August 1988	BBC SO BBC Singers Cuberli, Dupuy, K.Lewis, Halfvarson, Kennedy	Unpublished radio broadcast

Norma, excerpt (Casta diva)

London 23 September 1958	Orchestra Callas	LP: Voce 18 CD: Legato LCD 162

ALBAN BERG (1885-1935)

Violin Concerto

Edinburgh August 1960	Liverpool PO Stern	Unpublished radio broadcast

LENNOX BERKELEY (1903-1989)

Symphony No 3

Cheltenham 6 July 1973	BBC SO	Unpublished radio broadcast

HECTOR BERLIOZ (1803-1869)

Symphonie fantastique

Liverpool Date not confirmed	Liverpool PO	Unpublished radio broadcast

Symphonie funèbre et triomphale

London 22 July 1983	BBC SO	Unpublished radio broadcast <u>Third movement</u> CD: BBC DMCD 98

Rêverie et caprice pour violon et orchestre

London 20 November 1960- March 1965	Philharmonia Menuhin	LP: HMV ALP 2070/ASD 618/SXLP 30249 CD: EMI CDM 763 5302

Béatrice et Bénédict, excerpt (Dieu! Que viens-je d'entendre?)

London 4-10 January 1976	LPO Stade	LP: CBS 76522 CD: Sony 39315

Benvenuto Cellini

London December 1966	Covent Garden Orchestra & Chorus Vaughan, Minton, Gedda, Massard	Unpublished radio broadcast <u>Seul pour lutter</u> LP: Ed Smith EJS 518

La damnation de Faust, excerpt (D'amour l'ardente flamme)

London 4-10 January 1976	LPO Stade	LP: CBS 76522 CD: Sony 39315

Les troyens, Royal Hunt and Storm

Barking 16-18 June 1969	LPO	LP: Pye TPLS 13032/GSGC 15002

HARRISON BIRTWISTLE (Born 1934)

The Triumph of Time

London 19 April 1982	BBC SO	Unpublished radio broadcast

ALEXANDER BORODIN (1833-1887)

Prince Igor, excerpt (Jaroslavna's aria)

Liverpool Date not confirmed	Liverpool PO Söderström	Unpublished radio broadcast

JOHANNES BRAHMS (1833-1897)

Symphony No 2

London 3 September 1981	BBC SO	CD: Radio Classics BBCRD 9113

Piano Concerto No 1

London 17 December 1982	BBC SO Leonskaja	Unpublished radio broadcast

Piano Concerto No 2

London 13 September 1972	New Philharmonia Watts	Unpublished radio broadcast

Academic Festival Overture

Bedford 22 March 1983	BBC SO	CD: Radio Classics BBCRD 9113

Tragic Overture

London 19 May 1983	BBC SO	CD: Radio Classics BBCRD 9113

BENJAMIN BRITTEN (1913-1976)

Peter Grimes

New York 10 December 1977	Metropolitan Opera Orchestra & Chorus Harper, Chookasian, Vickers, Gramm	Unpublished Met broadcast

Cello Symphony

London 10 January 1980	BBC SO Lloyd-Webber	Unpublished radio broadcast

Violin Concerto

Croydon 13-15 April 1974	LPO Friend	LP: EMI CFP 4489/CFP 40068/CFP 40250

Serenade for tenor, horn and strings

Croydon 19 December 1974	LPO Partridge, Busch	LP: EMI CFP 40250

Young Persons' Guide to the Orchestra

London 30 July 1974	BBC SO	Unpublished radio broadcast
London 11 August 1976	BBC Philharmonic	Unpublished radio broadcast

ANTON BRUCKNER (1824-1896)

Overture in G minor

London 11 August 1976	BBC Philharmonic	Unpublished radio broadcast

FERRUCCIO BUSONI (1866-1924)

Arlecchino

Glyndebourne 16 July 1954	RPO Gester, M.Dickie, Wallace, G.Evans, Ollendorff	Unpublished radio broadcast
London 17-20 July 1954	RPO Gester, M.Dickie, Wallace, G.Evans, Ollendorff	LP: HMV ALP 1223 LP: Victor LM 1944 CD: EMI CMS 565 2842
Edinburgh September 1960	RPO Pilarczyk, Troy, Wallace, Blankenburg	CD: Opera Society OSCD 225
Glyndebourne August 1965	LPO Venora, M.Dickie, Wicks, Blankenburg	Unpublished video recording

Comedy Overture

Liverpool Date not confirmed	Liverpool PO	Unpublished radio broadcast

JOSEPH CANTELOUBE (1879-1957)

Chants d'Auvergne

London 9-12 December 1988	Philharmonia Roszario	CD: Pickwick PCD 938 <u>Excerpts</u> CD: Pickwick PCD 1090/PCDS 22

EMMANUEL CHABRIER (1841-1894)

Espana

Barking 4 April 1971	LPO	LP: EMI CFP 169

FRANCIS CHAGRIN (1905-1972)

Helter Skelter, overture

London 11 January 1976	LPO	LP: Lyrita SRCS 95

ERNEST CHAUSSON (1855-1899)

Poème pour violon et orchestre

London 22 November- 16 December 1960	Philharmonia Menuhin	LP: HMV ALP 2070/ASD 618/SXLP 30249 CD: EMI CDM 763 5302

FREDERIC CHOPIN (1810-1849)

Piano Concerto No 2

Watford 11-13 January 1966	Philharmonia Rosen	LP: Columbia CX 5273/SAX 5273 LP: CBS 61094 CD: Sony SBK 46336 Third movement LP: Columbia (USA) 6P-6209

DOMENICO CIMAROSA (1749-1801)

Il matrimonio segreto

Edinburgh 25 August 1980	Scottish CO Daniels, Lak, Szirmay, Saeder, Kuebler, Runger	Unpublished radio broadcast

Il maestro di cappella, intermezzo giocoso for baritone and orchestra

London 24 August 1963	LPO Feller	Unpublished radio broadcast

AARON COPLAND (1900-1990)

El salón México

Croydon 23-24 February 1975	LPO	LP: EMI CFP 40240 CD: EMI CDCFP 4537/CDCFP 9019

ARCANGELO CORELLI (1653-1713)

Concerto in G minor "Christmas Concerto"

Vienna 23 March- 30 April 1953	Vienna SO	LP: Philips A00668R/ABR 4014

CLAUDE DEBUSSY (1862-1918)

3 Nocturnes

Edinburgh August 1961	LSO Edinburgh Choral Union	Unpublished radio broadcast

Ibéria (Images pour orchestre)

Cheltenham 6 July 1973	BBC SO	Unpublished radio broadcast

Prélude à l'après-midi d'un faune

Barking 16-18 June 1969	LPO	LP: Pye TPLS 13032/GSGC 15002/GH 670

L'enfant prodigue, excerpt (L'année en vain chasse l'année)

New York 22 October 1983	Metropolitan Opera Orchestra Cotrubas	Unpublished Met broadcast and unpublished video recording <u>Performed at the Met centennial gala</u>

LEO DELIBES (1836-1891)

Lakmé, excerpt (Viens Mallika!)

New York 22 October 1983	Metropolitan Opera Orchestra Devia, Kraft	Unpublished Met broadcast and unpublished video recording <u>Performed at the Met centennial gala</u>

FREDERICK DELIUS (1862-1934)

Piano Concerto

London 3 September 1981	BBC SO Curzon	Unpublished radio broadcast

Dance Rhapsody No 1

London 30 July 1974	BBC SO	Unpublished radio broadcast

Summer Night on the River

London 18 April 1984	BBC SO	CD: Radio Classics 15656 91332

ERNO DOHNANYI (1877-1960)

Piano Concerto No 1

London 8-9 December 1971	New Philharmonia Vaszonyi	LP: Pye TPLS 13052/GSGC 2052 CD: Precision PVCD 8398

GAETONO DOHNANYI (1797-1848)

Don Pasquale, excerpt (So anch'io la virtù magica)

London 24 February- 4 December 1976	New Philharmonia Cotrubas	LP: CBS 76521

Don Pasquale, excerpt (Signorina in tanta fretta)

New York 22 October 1983	Metropolitan Opera Orchestra Daniels, Tajo	Unpublished Met broadcast and unpublished video recording <u>Performed at the Met centennial gala</u>

L'elisir d'amore

London January 1977	Covent Garden Orchestra & Chorus Cotrubas, Watson, Domingo, G.Evans, Wixell	LP: CBS 79210 CD: Sony 79210 <u>Excerpts</u> CD: Sony 74022

Emilia di Liverpool, abridged version

Liverpool 8 September 1957	Liverpool PO and Chorus Sutherland, Cantelo, McAlpine, Dowling, Alan	LP: Ed Smith EJS 161 LP: Voce 30 CD: Myto MCD 91546

Lucia di Lammermoor

Rome July- August 1961	Santa Cecilia Orchestra & Chorus Sutherland, Satre, Cioni, MacDonald, Merrill, Siepi	LP: Decca MET 212-214/SET 212-214/ GOM 663-665/GOS 663-665 CD: Decca 411 6222 <u>Excerpts</u> LP: Decca LXT 5684/SXL 2315 CD: Decca 417 7802
Edinburgh August 1961	Covent Garden Orchestra & Chorus Sutherland, Elkins, Turp, MacDonald, Shaw, Rouleau	Unpublished radio broadcast

HENRI DUPARC (1848-1933)

Mélodies: L'invitation au voyage; La vie antérieure; Le manoir de Rosamonde; Testament; Au pays où se fait la guerre; Chanson triste

Brussels 29 June- 3 July 1983	Monnaie Orchestra Kanawa	LP: EMI EL 27 01351 CD: EMI CDC 747 1112

ANTONIN DVORAK (1841-1904)

Rusalka, excerpt (O silver moon!)

London 12-15 November 1987	Philharmonia Mattila	LP: Philips 422 0731 CD: Philips 422 0732

EDWARD ELGAR (1857-1934)

The Dream of Gerontius

Liverpool Date not confirmed	Liverpool PO Huddersfield Choral Society <u>Soloists included</u> M.Thomas, R.Lewis	Unpublished radio broadcast

Symphony No 1

London 16 August 1983	BBC SO	CD: Radio Classics BBCRD 9121

Violin Concerto

London 1981	BBC SO Haendel	CD: Radio Classics awaiting publication

In the South, concert overture

London 30 July 1974	BBC SO	CD: Radio Classics BBCRD 9121

In the original Italian

Così fan tutte

ossia

La scuola degli amanti

OPERA BUFFA IN DUE ATTI

Poesia di Lorenzo da Ponte   Musica di W. A. Mozart

Conductor: JOHN PRITCHARD   Producer: CARL EBERT

Scenery designed by ROLF GÉRARD

Costumes designed by BERNARD NEVILL

THE ROYAL PHILHARMONIC ORCHESTRA

THE GLYNDEBOURNE FESTIVAL CHORUS

Scenery built by THE RINGMER BUILDING WORKS LTD. *under the supervision of*
R. W. GOUGH *and* S. ZEAL

Scenery painted under the supervision of CHARLES BRAVERY *and* DAVID HOMAN

Costumes made by the GLYNDEBOURNE OPERA WARDROBE
under the supervision of ROSEMARY WILKINS

Tailoring by BONN & MACKENZIE LTD.   *Principals' hats by* HUGH SKILLEN

Wigs by WIG CREATIONS   *Shoes by* ANELLO & DAVIDE

Properties made at GLYNDEBOURNE *under the supervision of* HARRY KELLARD

Cast

Ferrando, *an officer, lover of Dorabella* .. .. Loren Driscoll *(American)*
Guglielmo, *an officer, lover of Fiordiligi* .. Ingvar Wixell *(Swedish)*
Don Alfonso, *an elderly philosopher* .. .. Michel Roux *(French)*
Fiordiligi, *a lady of Ferrara* .. .. .. Antigone Sgourda *(Greek)*
Dorabella, *her sister* .. .. .. Stefania Malagù *(Italian)*
Despina, *maid to the ladies* .. .. .. Reri Grist *(American)*

Continuo played by the Conductor

The scene is laid in the neighbourhood of Naples

ACT I

Scene I   A tavern
Scene II   The garden of the sisters' villa
Scene III   A room in the villa
Scene IV   The garden

DINNER INTERVAL OF APPROXIMATELY 75 MINUTES

ACT II

Scene I   Another room in the villa
Scene II   The garden
Scene III   A pavilion
Scene IV   A terrace

Dates of Performance: June 15 · 17 · 19 · 23 · 25 · July 2 · 4 · 6 · 8 · 12 · 14 · 18 · 20 · 22 · 26

The Audience is particularly requested to refrain from applauding until the music has stopped at the end of a scene or aria.

CESAR FRANCK (1822-1890)

Variations symphoniques pour piano et orchestre

London 24 August 1963	LPO Lythgoe	Unpublished radio broadcast

PETER RACINE FRICKER (1920-1990)

Symphony No 2

Liverpool 13-14 August 1954	Liverpool PO	LP: HMV DLP 1080/HQM 1010 <u>Excerpt</u> CD: EMI CDM 763 3702

GEORGE GERSHWIN (1898-1937)

An American in Paris

Croydon 23-24 February 1975	LPO	LP: EMI CFP 40240 CD: EMI CDCFP 4537/CDCFP 9019

Porgy and Bess, suite arranged by Bennett

Croydon 23-24 February 1975	LPO	LP: EMI CFP 40240 CD: EMI CDCFP 4537/CDCFP 9019

CHARLES GOUNOD (1818-1893)

Faust, excerpt (O dieu, que de bijoux!)

London 12-15 November 1987	Philharmonia Mattila	LP: Philips 422 0731 CD: Philips 422 0732

Roméo et Juliette, excerpt (Depuis hier je cherche)

London 4-10 January 1976	LPO Stade	LP: CBS 76522 CD: Sony SK 39315

EDVARD GRIEG (1843-1907)

Piano Concerto

Barking 16-17 June 1970	LPO Katin	LP: EMI CFP 160/1A 197 54430-54433/ 1C 027 05679

Peer Gynt, excerpts

Barking 7 January 1971	LPO	LP: EMI CFP 160/1C 027 05679 MM 30015

IAIN HAMILTON (Born 1922)

Circus for 2 trumpets and orchestra

London 21 January 1970	BBC SO P.Jones, Howarth	Unpublished radio broadcast

GEORGE FRIDERIC HANDEL (1685-1759)

Concerto grosso op 6 no 1

Vienna 9-13 April 1954	Vienna SO	LP: Philips A00235L/ABL 3075

Concerto grosso op 6 no 2

Vienna 9-13 April 1954	Vienna SO	LP: Philips A00235L/ABL 3075

Concerto grosso op 6 no 6

Vienna 9-13 April 1954	Vienna SO	LP: Philips A00235L/ABL 3075

Concerto grosso op 6 no 7

Vienna 9-13 April 1954	Vienna SO	LP: Philips A00235L/ABL 3075

Concerto grosso op 6 no 12

Vienna 23 March- 30 April 1953	Vienna SO	LP: Philips S06105R/ABR 4014

Messiah, selection

London 1-2 April 1963	LPO Harper, Procter, Holmes, Lewis	LP: Readers' Digest

Let thy hand be strengthened, Coronation anthem

Huddersfield 1977	Northern Sinfonia Huddersfield Choral Society	LP: Enigma K 53542 LP: ASV ACM 2041

My heart is inditing, Coronation anthem

Huddersfield 1977	Northern Sinfonia Huddersfield Choral Society	LP: Enigma K 53542 LP: ASV ACM 2041 Third movement CD: ASV CDQS 6010

The King shall rejoice, Coronation anthem

Huddersfield 1977	Northern Sinfonia Huddersfield Choral Society	LP: Enigma K 53542 LP: ASV ACM 2041 Second movement CD: ASV CDQS 6010

Zadok the Priest, Coronation anthem

Huddersfield 1977	Northern Sinfonia Huddersfield Choral Society	LP: Enigma K 53542 LP: ASV ACM 2041 CD: ASV CDQS 6036

FRANZ JOSEF HAYDN (1732-1809)

Symphony No 44 "Trauer"

Watford 10-11 February 1973	LPO	LP: EMI CFP 40021

Symphony No 45 "Farewell"

Watford 10-11 February 1973	LPO	LP: EMI CFP 40021

Symphony No 52

London 12 August 1972	BBC SO	Unpublished radio broadcast

Symphony No 80

London 20-21 December 1954	Philharmonia	LP: HMV CLP 1061

Symphony No 85 "La reine"

London   BBC SO   Unpublished radio broadcast
14 August
1971

Symphony No 95

Edinburgh   Liverpool PO   Unpublished radio broadcast
August
1960

Notturno No 6 for wind and strings

London   Philharmonia   LP: HMV CLP 1061
20-21
December
1954

HANS WERNER HENZE (Born 1926)

Elegy for young lovers

London 15 July 1961	RPO Dorow, Söderström, Meyer, Turp, Hemsley, Alexander	Unpublished radio broadcast

RICHARD HEUBERGER (1850-1914)

Der Opernball, excerpt (Ins chambre séparée)

London 14 August 1971	BBC SO C.Wilson, Burrows	CD: Radio Classics BBCRD 9109

PAUL HINDEMITH (1895-1963)

Der Schwanendreher, concerto after folksongs for viola and orchestra

Walthamstow 8-9 December 1953	Orchestra Primrose	LP: Philips ABL 3045

GUSTAV HOLST (1874-1934)

Hymn of Jesus

London 30 July 1974	BBC SO BBC Chorus	Unpublished radio broadcast

ENGELBERT HUMPERDINCK (1854-1921)

Hänsel und Gretel

Cologne June- July 1978	Gürzenich Orchestra Cologne Opera Chorus Cotrubas, Kanawa, Stade, Welting, C.Ludwig, Söderström, Nimsgern	LP: CBS 79217 CD: Sony M2K 79217 <u>Excerpt</u> CD: Sony 39208

JOSIF IVANOVICI (1845-1902)

Donauwellen, waltz

Walthamstow 8 December 1961	LPO	LP: Pye GGL 0127/GSGL 10127/MAL 571

FRANZ LEHAR (1870-1948)

Giuditta, excerpt (Du bist meine Sonne)

London 14 August 1971	BBC SO Burrows	CD: Radio Classics BBCRD 9109

Die lustige Witwe, excerpt (Viljalied)

London 14 August 1971	BBC SO C.Wilson	CD: Radio Classics BBCRD 9109
London 12 August 1972	BBC SO C.Wilson	Unpublished radio broadcast

Gold und Silber, waltz

Walthamstow 8 December 1961	LPO	LP: Pye GGL 0127/GSGL 10127
London 14 August 1971	BBC SO	CD: Radio Classics BBCRD 9109

FRANZ LISZT (1811-1886)

Piano Concerto No 1

Liverpool Date not confirmed	Liverpool PO Ogdon	Unpublished radio broadcast
Watford 11-13 January 1966	Philharmonia Rosen	LP: Columbia CX 5273/SAX 5273 LP: CBS 61094 CD: Sony SBK 45504

Piano Concerto No 2

London November 1966	Pro Arte Orchestra Siki	LP: Pye GGC 4054/GSGC 14054

Hungarian Fantasy for piano and orchestra

London 22 December 1963	Philharmonia Ogdon	LP: HMV ALP 2051/ASD 600/SLS 5033 LP: World Records T 697/ST 697

Rapsodie espagnole for piano and orchestra, arranged by Busoni

London 22 December 1963	Philharmonia Ogdon	LP: HMV ALP 2051/ASD 600 LP: World Records T 697/ST 697

HENRY LITOLFF (1818-1891)

Scherzo (Concerto symphonique no 4)

Barking 16-17 June 1970	LPO Katin	LP: EMI CFP 115

EDWARD MACDOWELL (1860-1908)

Piano Concerto No 2

London 24 August 1963	LPO Lythgoe	Unpublished radio broadcast

FRANCESCO MANFREDINI (1684-1762)

Sinfonia pastorale per il santissimo natale

Vienna 23 March- 30 April 1954	Vienna SO	LP: Philips A00668R/ABR 4014

JULES MASSENET (1842-1912)

Thaïs

New York 28 January 1978	Metropolitan Opera Orchestra & Chorus Sills, I.Jones, Gibbs, Milnes	Unpublished Met broadcast

Cendrillon, excerpt (Enfin je suis ici!)

London 4-10 January 1976	LPO Stade	LP: CBS 76522 CD: Sony 39315

Werther, excerpt (Laisse couler les larmes!)

London 4-10 January 1976	LPO Stade	LP: CBS 76522 CD: Sony 39315

FELIX MENDELSSOHN-BARTHOLDY (1809-1847)

A Midsummer Night's Dream, Wedding march and nocturne

| Watford 13 January 1966 | Philharmonia | CBS unpublished |

GIACOMO MEYERBEER (1791-1864)

Les Huguenots, excerpt (Nobles seigneurs!)

| London 4-10 January 1976 | LPO Stade | LP: CBS 76522 CD: Sony 39315 |

CARL MILLOECKER (1842-1899)

Die Dubarry, excerpt (Ich schenk' mein Herz)

| London 12 August 1972 | BBC SO C.Wilson | Unpublished radio broadcast |

ANTHONY MILNER (Born 1925)

Symphony

London 17 January 1973	BBC SO	Unpublished radio broadcast <u>Premiere performance</u>

CLAUDIO MONTEVERDI (1567-1643)

L'incoronazione di Poppea

London 1 July- 8 August 1963	RPO Glyndebourne Festival Chorus Laszlo, Bible, Marimpietri, Dominguez, R.Lewis, Cava, Alberti	LP: EMI AN 126-127/SAN 126-127/SLS 5248 LP: Angel 3644/6073 <u>Excerpts</u> LP: EMI SEOM 3 CD: EMI CDH 565 0722
London 29 July 1963	RPO Glyndebourne Festival Chorus Laszlo, Bible, Marimpietri, Dominguez, R.Lewis, Cava, Alberti	Unpublished radio broadcast

WOLFGANG AMADEUS MOZART (1756-1791)

Symphony No 31 "Paris"

Edinburgh August 1961	LSO	Unpublished radio broadcast

Symphony No 39

London 17 January 1983	BBC SO	Unpublished radio broadcast

Symphony No 40

London 3 September 1981	BBC SO	CD: Radio Classics BBCRD 9112
London 20 January 1983	BBC SO	Unpublished radio broadcast

Symphony No 41 "Jupiter"

London 22 January 1983	BBC SO	Unpublished radio broadcast

Piano Concerto No 17

Vienna 7 April 1954	Vienna SO Henkemans	LP: Philips A00239L/695 036KL

Piano Concerto No 18

Vienna 17-24 March 1953	Vienna SO Henkemans	LP: Philips A00184L

Piano Concerto No 19

Vienna 17-24 March 1953	Vienna SO Henkemans	LP: Philips A00184L

Piano Concerto No 21

London 17 January 1983	BBC SO Klien	Unpublished radio broadcast

Piano Concerto No 22

London 14 August 1971	BBC SO Roll	CD: Radio Classics BBCRD 9112

Piano Concerto No 23

London 20 January 1983	BBC SO Klien	Unpublished radio broadcast

Piano Concerto No 24

London 22 January 1983	BBC SO Klien	Unpublished radio broadcast

Piano Concerto No 27

Vienna 8 April 1954	Vienna SO Henkemans	LP: Philips A00239L/693 036KL

Violin Concerto No 4

London 6 December 1954	Philharmonia Menuhin	LP: HMV ALP 1281 LP: Electrola E 90112/WALP 1281

Violin Concerto No 5

London 6 January 1954	Philharmonia Menuhin	LP: HMV ALP 1281 LP: Electrola E 90112/WALP 1281

Flute Concerto No 1

Vienna 28-29 January 1953	Vienna SO Barwahser	LP: Philips A00166L/ABL 3059/6530 046

Flute Concerto No 2

Vienna 28-29 January 1953	Vienna SO Barwahser	LP: Philips A00166L/ABL 3059/6530 046

Serenade No 6 "Serenata notturna"

London 20-21 December 1954	Philharmonia	LP: HMV CLP 1061

Serenade No 13 "Eine kleine Nachtmusik"

London   BBC SO   CD: Radio Classics BBCRD 9112
10 January
1980

Maurerische Trauermusik

London   New Philharmonia   Unpublished radio broadcast
13 September
1972

Bastien und Bastienne

Vienna   Vienna SO   LP: Philips A00167L/ABL 3010
25-31   I.Hollweg,
January   Kmennt, Berry
1953

Ch'io mi scordi di te?, concert aria

London   LSO   LP: Decca LXT 6045/SXL 6045/
15-21   Berganza   ADD 176/SDD 176
December   Parsons, piano   CD: Decca 421 8992
1962

La clemenza di Tito, excerpt (Parto, parto!)

London   LSO   LP: Decca LXT 6045/SXL 6045/
15-21   Berganza   ADD 176/SDD 176
December   CD: Decca 421 8992
1962

Così fan tutte

Glyndebourne 17 July 1959	RPO Glyndebourne Festival Chorus Ligabue, Lane, Sciutti, Oncina, Feller, Bruscantini	Unpublished radio broadcast
New York 22 January 1972	Metropolitan Opera Orchestra & Chorus Zylis-Gara, Elias, Stratas, Uppmann, Bottazzo, Corena	Unpublished Met broadcast
Glyndebourne August 1975	LPO Glyndebourne Festival Chorus Döse, Lindenstrand, Perriers, A.Austin, Allen, F.Petri	VHS Video: Pickwick SL 2002

Così fan tutte, excerpt (Come scoglio)

London 15-21 December 1962	LSO Berganza	LP: Decca LXT 6045/SXL 6045/ ADD 176/SDD 176 CD: Decca 421 8992

Così fan tutte, excerpt (Per pietà)

London 15-21 December 1962	LSO Berganza	LP: Decca LXT 6045/SXL 6045/ ADD 176/SDD 176 CD: Decca 421 8992

Così fan tutte, excerpt (E amore un ladroncello)

London 15-21 December 1962	LSO Berganza	LP: Decca LXT 6045/SXL 6045/ ADD 176/SDD 176 CD: Decca 421 8992

Così fan tutte, excerpt (Un aura amorosa)

London 21-22 February 1973	LSO Burrows	LP: Decca DSLO 13/410 1431

Così fan tutte, excerpt (Ah lo veggio!)

London 19-21 June 1974	LPO Burrows	LP: Decca DSLO 13/410 1431

Così fan tutte, excerpt (In qual fiero contrasto)

London 21-22 February 1973	LSO Burrows	LP: Decca DSLO 13/410 1431

Davidde penitente, excerpt (Tra l'oscure ombre funeste)

Paris 17 December 1964	Orchestre National Stich-Randall	CD: Chant du monde LDC 278.887

Don Giovanni

Glyndebourne October 1967	RPO Glyndebourne Festival Chorus Bridges, Zylis-Gara, Armstrong, R.Lewis, Paskalis, Montarsolo, Rintzler	Unpublished video recording

Don Giovanni, excerpt (Mi tradì)

London 12-15 November 1987	Philharmonia Mattila	LP: Philips 422 0731 CD: Philips 422 0732

Don Giovanni, excerpt (Non mi dir)

London 4 July 1952	Philharmonia Schwarzkopf	45: Columbia SEL 1515 LP: Columbia 33CX 1069 LP: Columbia (Germany) C 90321 LP: Angel 35021 LP: World Records T 583 LP: EMI RLS 763/2C 051 43222 CD: EMI CDC 747 9502/CDH 763 7082 CD: NotaBlu 935.0911

Don Giovanni, excerpt (Batti batti)

London 1 July 1952	Philharmonia Schwarzkopf	78: Columbia LB 145 45: Columbia SEL 1511 LP: Columbia 33CX 1069 LP: Columbia (Germany) C 90321 LP: Angel 35021 LP: World Records T 583 LP: EMI 2C 051 43222 CD: EMI CDC 747 9502/CDH 763 7082

Don Giovanni, excerpt (Vedrai carino)

London 2 July 1952	Philharmonia Schwarzkopf	78: Columbia LB 145 45: Columbia SEL 1511 LP: Columbia 33CX 1069 LP: Columbia (Germany) C 90321 LP: Angel 35021 LP: World Records T 583 LP: EMI 2C 051 43222 CD: EMI CDC 747 9502/CDH 763 7082

Don Giovanni, excerpt (Là ci darem la mano)

New York 22 October 1983	Metropolitan Opera Orchestra M.Merritt, Cheek	Unpublished Met broadcast and unpublished video recording <u>Performed at the Met centennial gala</u>

Don Giovanni, excerpt (Il mio tesoro)

London 19-21 June 1974	LPO Burrows	LP: Decca DSLO 13/410 1431

Don Giovanni, excerpt (Dalla sua pace)

London 19-21 June 1974	LPO Burrows	LP: Decca DSLO 13/410 1431

Die Entführung aus dem Serail

Salzburg August 1967	VPO Vienna Opera Chorus Hallstein, Grist, Alva, Unger, Corena	Unpublished radio broadcast
Glyndebourne August 1972	LPO Glyndebourne Festival Chorus M.Price, Perriers, R.Davies, Lappalainen, Mangin	Unpublished video recording

Die Entführung aus dem Serail, excerpts

Glyndebourne 22-24 July 1972	LPO M.Price, Perriers, R.Davies, Lappalainen, Mangin	LP: EMI CFP 40032/1C 047 50584 LP: Vanguard VSD 71023 Excerpts CD: EMI CDH 565 0722

Die Entführung aus dem Serail, excerpt (Martern aller Arten)

London 12-15 November 1987	Philharmonia Mattila	LP: Philips 422 0731 CD: Philips 422 0732

Die Entführung aus dem Serail, excerpt (Ach, ich liebte!)

London 24 February- 4 December 1976	New Philharmonia Cotrubas	LP: CBS 76521

Die Entführung aus dem Serail, excerpt (Hier soll ich dich denn sehen?)

London	LSO	LP: Decca DSLO 13/410 1431
21-23	Burrows	
February		
1973		

Die Entführung aus dem Serail, excerpt (O wie ängstlich!)

London	LSO	LP: Decca DSLO 13/410 1431
21-23	Burrows	
February		
1973		

Die Entführung aus dem Serail, excerpt (Wenn der Freude Tränen fliessen)

London	LSO	LP: Decca DSLO 13/410 1431
21-23	Burrows	
February		
1973		

Die Entführung aus dem Serail, excerpt (Ich baue ganz)

London	LSO	LP: Decca DSLO 13/410 1431
21-23	Burrows	
February		
1973		

Exsultate jubilate

London	Philharmonia	Columbia unpublished
15-16	Schwarzkopf	
September		
1952		

Idomeneo

London 6 July– 27 August 1956	RPO Glyndebourne Festival Chorus Jurinac, Udovick, Simoneau, R.Lewis, Milligan, McAlpine	LP: HMV ALP 1515-1517 LP: Angel 3574/6070 LP: World Records OC 201-203/ SOC 201-203 CD: EMI CHS 763 6852 Excerpts LP: HMV ALP 1731 LP: Angel 35595 LP: World Records OH 204/SOH 204 CD: EMI CDH 565 0722
Glyndebourne July 1964	LPO Glyndebourne Festival Chorus Janowitz, Tarres, R.Lewis, Pavarotti, Wicks	CD: Butterfly BMCD 010 Excerpts CD: Opera CD 54039
London 17 August 1964	LPO Glyndebourne Festival Chorus Janowitz, Tarres, R.Lewis, Pavarotti, Wicks	LP: Historical Recording Enterprises HRE 364 LP: Melodram MEL 032 CD: Melodram MEL 27003 CD: Verona 27038-27039 CD: NotaBlu 920.715 Excerpts CD: NotaBlu 920.711
Glyndebourne August 1974	LPO Glyndebourne Festival Chorus Betley, Barstow, R.Lewis, Goeke, Wicks	VHS Video: Pickwick SL 2003
Vienna 20 June– 23 September 1983	VPO Vienna Opera Chorus Popp, Gruberova, Baltsa, Pavarotti, Nucci	LP: Decca 411 8051 CD: Decca 411 8052 Excerpts CD: Decca 430 1202

Thursday, 11th December, 1952

The 131st performance at the Royal Opera House

of

THE MAGIC FLUTE

OPERA IN TWO ACTS

Words by Emanuel Schikaneder and Karl Ludwig Giesecke

Music by Wolfgang Amadeus Mozart

English version by Edward J. Dent

Costumes, settings and visual effects devised by Oliver Messel

CONDUCTOR - JOHN PRITCHARD

THE COVENT GARDEN OPERA CHORUS
Chorus Master · Douglas Robinson

THE COVENT GARDEN ORCHESTRA
Leader - Charles Taylor

WOLFGANG AMADEUS MOZART, 1756 - 1791

This opera was first produced on 30th September, 1791, at the Theater auf der Wieden, Vienna. First performed in London, in Italian, at the Haymarket Theatre on 6th June, 1811. First performed in English at Norwich in 1829 and in London at Drury Lane on 10th March, 1838. This opera was first performed at the Royal Opera House on 27th May, 1833.

CHARACTERS IN ORDER OF APPEARANCE

TAMINO, an Egyptian Prince	JOHN LANIGAN
FIRST LADY ⎫	JOAN SUTHERLAND
SECOND LADY ⎬ attending the Queen of Night	JANET HOWE
THIRD LADY ⎭	JEAN WATSON
PAPAGENO, a bird catcher	JESS WALTERS
THE QUEEN OF THE NIGHT	ILSE HOLLWEG
FIRST BOY ⎫	APRIL CANTELO
SECOND BOY ⎬ Genii of the Temple	LEONNE MILLS
THIRD BOY ⎭	BARBARA HOWITT
MONOSTATOS, a Moor in Sarastro's service	ANTHONY MARLOWE
PAMINA, daughter of the Queen of Night	ADELE LEIGH
THE SPEAKER OF THE TEMPLE	GERAINT EVANS
SARASTRO, High Priest of the Temple	INIA TE WIATA
FIRST PRIEST	WILLIAM MCALPINE
SECOND PRIEST	BRYAN DRAKE
THIRD PRIEST	HEDWORTH FISHER
FOURTH PRIEST	RONALD FIRMAGER
PAPAGENA, Papageno's sweetheart	NORAH CANNELL
FIRST MAN IN ARMOUR	THORSTEINN HANNESSON
SECOND MAN IN ARMOUR	RHYDDERCH DAVIES

The Childrens' chorus are members of the Kingsland Central School and have been trained by Mr. George Hurren.

Jean Watson appears by permission of the Governors of Sadler's Wells

Idomeneo, excerpt (Zeffiretti lusinghieri)

London 10 September 1952	Philharmonia Schwarzkopf	45: Columbia SEL 1515 LP: Columbia 33CX 1069 LP: Columbia (Germany) C 90321 LP: Angel 35021 LP: World Records T 583 LP: EMI 2C 051 43222 CD: EMI CDC 747 9502/CDH 763 7082

Idomeneo, excerpt (Fuor del mar)

London 21-23 February 1973	LSO Burrows	LP: Decca DSLO 13/410 1431

Nehmt meinen Dank, concert aria

Vienna 11-13 April 1953	Vienna SO I.Hollweg	LP: Philips A00657R/ABR 4054

Non temer amato bene, concert aria

London 15-21 December 1962	LSO Berganza	LP: Decca LXT 6045/SXL 6045/ADD 176/ SDD 176/D251 D5 CD: Decca 421 8992/430 3002

Le nozze di Figaro

Glyndebourne August 1973	LPO Glyndebourne Festival Chorus Kanawa, Cotrubas, Stade, Skram, Luxon	VHS Video: Longman LGVH 7013 VHS Video: Pickwick SLL 7013
London August 1974	LPO Glyndebourne Festival Chorus Kanawa, Gale, Jungwirth-Ahnsjö, Skram, Devlin	Unpublished radio broadcast

Le nozze di Figaro, overture

Vienna 20-22 March 1989	VPO	CD: Decca 430 2072/452 6242

Le nozze di Figaro, excerpt (Dove sono)

London 1 July 1952	Philharmonia Schwarzkopf	LP: Columbia 33CX 1069 LP: Columbia (Germany) C 90321 LP: Angel 35021 LP: World Records T 583 LP: EMI RLS 763/2C 051 43222 CD: EMI CDH 763 7082 CD: NotaBlu 935.0911
Liverpool Date not confirmed	Liverpool PO Söderström	Unpublished radio broadcast

Le nozze di Figaro, excerpt (Dove sono)

London 9 September 1952	Philharmonia Schwarzkopf	LP: Columbia 33CX 1069 LP: Columbia (Germany) C 90321 LP: Angel 35021 LP: World Records T 583 LP: EMI RLS 763/2C 051 43222 CD: EMI CDH 763 7082
Liverpool Date not confirmed	Liverpool PO Söderström	Unpublished radio broadcast

Le nozze di Figaro, excerpt (Deh vieni non tardar)

London 2 July 1952	Philharmonia Schwarzkopf	LP: Columbia 33CX 1069 LP: Columbia (Germany) C 90321 LP: Angel 35021 LP: World Records T 583 LP: EMI RLS 763/2C 051 43222 CD: EMI CDC 747 6502/CDH 763 7082/ CDM 565 5772 CD: NotaBlu 935.0911
London 24 February- 4 December 1976	New Philharmonia Cotrubas	LP: CBS 76521

Le nozze di Figaro, excerpt (Non so più)

London 2 July 1952	Philharmonia Schwarzkopf	LP: Columbia 33CX 1069 LP: Columbia (Germany) C 90321 LP: Angel 35021 LP: World Records T 583 LP: EMI 2C 051 43222 CD: EMI CDC 747 6502/CDH 763 7082
London 15-21 December 1962	LSO Berganza	LP: Decca LXT 6045/SXL 6045/ ADD 176/SDD 176 CD: Decca 421 8992

Le nozze di Figaro, excerpt (Voi che sapete)

London 1 July 1952	Philharmonia Schwarzkopf	LP: Columbia 33CX 1069 LP: Columbia (Germany) C 90321 LP: Angel 35021 LP: World Records T 583 LP: EMI 2C 051 43222 CD: EMI CDC 747 6502/CDH 763 7082
London 15-21 December 1962	LSO Berganza	LP: Decca LXT 6045/SXL 6045/ ADD 176/SDD 176 CD: Decca 421 8992

Popoli di Tessaglia, concert aria

Vienna   Vienna SO   LP: Philips A00657R/ABR 4054
11-13   I.Hollweg
April
1953

Der Schauspieldirektor

Vienna   VPO   CD: Decca 430 2072/452 6242
20-22   Kanawa, Gruberova,
March   Heilmann, Jungwirth
1989

Il sogno di Scipione, excerpt (Ah perchè cercare deggio?)

Paris   Orchestre   CD: Chant du monde LDC 278.887
17 December   National
1964   Stich-Randall

Voi avete un cor fedele, concert aria

Vienna   Vienna SO   LP: Philips A00657R/ABR 4054
11-13   I.Hollweg
April
1953

Vorrei spiegarvi o Dio!, concert aria

Vienna 11-13 April 1953	Vienna SO I.Hollweg	LP: Philips A00657R/ABR 4054

Zaide, excerpt (Ruhe sanft, mein holdes Leben!)

London 12-15 November 1987	Philharmonia Mattila	LP: Philips 422 0731 CD: Philips 422 0732

Die Zauberflöte

Aix-en- Provence July 1963	Conservatoire Orchestra & Chorus Janowitz, D'Angelo, McAlpine, Mars, Tadeo	Unpublished video recording
Cologne June 1978	Gürzenich Orchestra & Chorus Perry, Sandoz, Winkler, Nicolai, Salminen, Stamm	Unpublished radio broadcast
New York 17 February 1979	Metropolitan Opera Orchestra & Chorus Mitchell, Sandoz, McCoy, Boesch, Monk, Stamm	Unpublished Met broadcast

Die Zauberflöte, excerpt (Ach, ich fühl's)

London 5 July 1952	Philharmonia Schwarzkopf	Columbia unpublished
London 24 February- 4 December 1976	New Philharmonia Cotrubas	LP: CBS 76521
London 12-15 November 1987	Philharmonia Mattila	LP: Philips 422 0731 CD: Philips 422 0732

Die Zauberflöte, excerpt (Dies Bildnis ist bezaubernd schön)

London 19-21 June 1974	LPO Burrows	LP: Decca DSLO 13/410 1431

Die Zauberflöte, excerpt (Wie stark ist nicht dein Zauberton)

London 19-21 June 1974	LPO Burrows	LP: Decca DSLO 13/410 1431

<u>Excerpts from Mozart operas were filmed at Glyndebourne in August 1956 for a BBC television documentary: Pritchard probably conducted some of these</u>

MODEST MUSSORGSKY (1839-1881)

Pictures from an exhibition, arranged by Ravel

Barking 19-22 June 1970	LPO	LP: EMI CFP 106/CFP 4554/CFP 40319 CD: EMI CDCFP 4554

LUIGI NONO (1924-1990)

Cantata sul ponte di Hiroshima

Edinburgh August 1961	LSO Edinburgh Choral Union Holden, Dorrow	Unpublished radio broadcast

JACQUES OFFENBACH (1819-1880)

La périchole, excerpt (Ah, quel diner!)

London 4-10 January 1976	LPO Stade	LP: CBS 76522 CD: Sony 39315

La grande duchesse de Gérolstein, excerpt (Dites-lui)

London 4-10 January 1976	LPO Stade	LP: CBS 76522 CD: Sony 39315

NICOLO PAGANINI (1782-1840)

Variations on Rossini's Di tanti palpiti

London 22 November 1960	Philharmonia Menuhin	HMV unpublished

SERGEI PROKOFIEV (1891-1953)

Romeo and Juliet, ballet suite

Barking 1-3 December 1975	LPO	LP: EMI CFP 40266

Peter and the Wolf

London 24 August 1963	LPO Slobodskaya, narrator	Unpublished radio broadcast

GIACOMO PUCCINI (1858-1924)

La Bohème, excerpt (Sì mi chiamano Mimì)

London 24 February- 4 December 1976	New Philharmonia Cotrubas	LP: CBS 76521

La Bohème, excerpt (Quando m'en vò)

London 17-21 September 1981	LPO Kanawa	LP: CBS 37298 CD: Sony 37298

La Bohème, excerpt (O Mimì, tu più non torni)

New York 22 October 1983	Metropolitan Opera Orchestra Winbergh, Hartman	Unpublished Met broadcast and unpublished video recording Performed at the Met centennial gala

Gianni Schicchi, excerpt (O mio babbino caro)

London 17-21 September 1981	LPO Kanawa	LP: CBS 37298 CD: Sony 37298

Madama Butterfly, excerpt (Un bel dì)

London 23 September 1958	Orchestra Callas	LP: Voce 18 CD: Legato LCD 162 Televised performance
London 17-21 September 1981	LPO Kanawa	LP: CBS 37298 CD: Sony 37298

Manon Lescaut, excerpt (In quelle trine morbide)

London 17-21 September 1981	LPO Kanawa	LP: CBS 37298 CD: Sony 37298

La rondine, excerpt (Folle amore)

London 24 February- 4 December 1976	New Philharmonia Cotrubas	LP: CBS 76521

La rondine, excerpt (Ch'e bel sogno di Doretta)

London 17-21 September 1981	LPO Kanawa	LP: CBS 37298 CD: Sony 37298

Tosca, excerpt (Vissi d'arte)

London 17 June 1958	Orchestra Callas	LP: Legendary LR 111 CD: Legato LCD 162 <u>Televised performance</u>
London 17-21 September 1981	LPO Kanawa	LP: CBS 37298 CD: Sony 37298

Turandot, excerpt (Tu che di gel sei cinta)

London 24 February– 4 December 1976	New Philharmonia Cotrubas	LP: CBS 76521

Le villi, excerpt (Se come voi piccina io fossi)

London 17-21 September 1981	LPO Kanawa	LP: CBS 37298 CD: Sony 37298

HENRY PURCELL (1659-1695)

Dido and Aeneas

Glyndebourne September 1965	LPO Glyndebourne Festival Chorus Baker, Robson, Minton, Hemsley	Unpublished video recording

SERGEI RACHMANINOV (1873-1943)

Piano Concerto No 2

London 29-30 January 1962	Philharmonia Ogdon	LP: HMV ALP 1928/ASD 492/SXLP 30552/ SLS 5033 CD: EMI CDM 763 5252

Piano Concerto No 3

London 8 February 1976	LPO Sheppard	LP: EMI CFP 40257

Rhapsody on a theme of Paganini

London 21-22 December 1963	Philharmonia Ogdon	HMV unpublished

ALAN RAWSTHORNE (1905-1971)

Symphony No 1

London 25 March 1975	LPO	LP: Lyrita SRCS 90

Piano Concerto No 2

Date not confirmed	BBC SO Ogdon	CD: Radio Classics 15656 91762

Concerto for 2 pianos and orchestra

London 14 August 1968	LPO Ogdon, Lucas	CD: Radio Classics 15656 91762

Symphonic Studies

London 11 January 1976	LPO	LP: Lyrita SRCS 90

Street Corner, overture

London 25 March 1975	LPO	LP: Lyrita SRCS 95

NIKOLAI RIMSKY-KORSAKOV (1844-1908)

Capriccio espagnol

Barking 4 April 1971	LPO	LP: EMI CFP 169

MAURICE RAVEL (1875-1937)

Alborada del gracioso

Edinburgh August 1960	Liverpool PO	Unpublished radio broadcast

L'heure espagnole

Glyndebourne October 1965	LPO Venora, Cuenod, Sénéchal	Unpublished video recording

Rapsodie espagnole

Barking 4 April 1971	LPO	LP: EMI CFP 169

Shéhérazade

Brussels 29 June- 2 July 1983	Monnaie Orchestra Kanawa	LP: EMI EL 27 01351 CD: EMI CDC 747 1112

GIOACHINO ROSSINI (1792-1868)

Il barbiere di Siviglia

New York 2 March 1974	Metropolitan Opera Orchestra & Chorus Elias, Love, Goeke, W.Walker	Unpublished Met broadcast

Il barbiere di Siviglia, excerpt (Una voce poco fà)

London 17 June 1958	Orchestra Callas	LP: Legendary LR 111 CD: Legato LCD 162 <u>Televised performance</u>

La cenerentola

Glyndebourne July 1960	RPO Glyndebourne Festival Chorus Pace, Rota, Zanolli, Oncina, Wallace, Bruscantini	Unpublished radio broadcast

La cenerentola, overture

London 24 August 1963	LPO	Unpublished radio broadcast

Le comte Ory

Glyndebourne August 1957	RPO Glyndebourne Festival Chorus Barabas,Sinclair, Oncina,Blankenburg	Unpublished video recording Act 2 only recorded
Glyndebourne July 1958	RPO Glyndebourne Festival Chorus Barabas,Sinclair, Oncina,Blankenburg	Unpublished radio broadcast

La gazza ladra

Wexford October 1959	Wexford Festival Orchestra & Chorus Adani, Baker, Bainbridge, Monti, Pedani, Anthony, Tadeo	LP: Ed Smith EJS 293 Abridged version, but first revival in twentieth century

Guillaume Tell, excerpt (Sombres forêts)

London 12-15 November 1987	Philharmonia Mattila	LP: Philips 422 0731 CD: Philips 422 0732

La pietra del paragone

Glyndebourne August 1965	LPO Glyndebourne Festival Chorus Valentini, Veasey, Reynolds, Roux, Blankenburg	Unpublished video recording

EDMUND RUBBRA (1901-1986)

Festival Te Deum

London 10 September 1952	RPO BBC Chorus Morison	Unpublished radio broadcast

FRANZ SCHUBERT (1797-1828)

Symphony No 3

London 17 January 1983	BBC SO	Unpublished radio broadcast
London 30 January 1983	BBC SO	Unpublished radio broadcast

Symphony No 4

London 20 January 1983	BBC SO	Unpublished radio broadcast

Symphony No 5

Watford 2-4 February 1975	LPO	LP: EMI CFP 40245/CFP 40370
London 22 January 1983	BBC SO	Unpublished radio broadcast

Symphony No 8 "Unfinished"

Walthamstow 8 December 1961	LPO	LP: Pye GGL 0212/GGL 0127/GSGL 10212/ GSGL 10127/MAL 552 LP: Europa E 120 LP: Audio Spectrum (USA) ASC 10003
Watford 2-4 February 1975	LPO	LP: EMI CFP 40245/CFP 40370

Symphony No 9 "Great"

Watford 3 March 1975	LPO	LP: EMI CFP 40233

German Dances, arranged by Webern

Liverpool Date not confirmed	Liverpool PO	Unpublished radio broadcast

ALEXANDER SCRIABIN (1872-1915)

Symphony No 3 "Divine poem"

London 1984	BBC SO	LP: BBC Records REGL 520 CD: BBC Records CD 520

ROGER SESSIONS (1896-1985)

Concerto for orchestra

London 17 December 1982	BBC SO	Unpublished radio broadcast

DIMITRI SHOSTAKOVICH (1906-1975)

Symphony No 11

London 12 April 1985	BBC SO	CD: Radio Classics 15656 91422

JEAN SIBELIUS (1865-1957)

Symphony No 2

Barking 16-18 June 1969	LPO	LP: Pye TPLS 13033/GSGC 15003

Valse triste

Walthamstow 8 December 1961	LPO	LP: Pye GGL 0127/GSGL 10127

In the original Italian

L'incoronazione di Poppea

DRAMMA IN MUSICA

Libretto di G. F. Busenello   Musica di Claudio Monteverdi

In a new version realised by Raymond Leppard

Conductor: JOHN PRITCHARD   Producer: GÜNTHER RENNERT

Scenery designed by HUGH CASSON

Costumes designed by CONWY EVANS

THE GLYNDEBOURNE FESTIVAL CHORUS AND BALLET

THE ROYAL PHILHARMONIC ORCHESTRA

Harpsichords played by RAYMOND LEPPARD *and* MARTIN ISEPP

Organs played by COURTNEY KENNY *and* FRANK SHIPWAY

Lute and Chitarrone: ROBERT SPENCER   *Guitar:* FREDDIE PHILLIPS

Harp: MARIA KORCHINSKA

Continuo 'Cello: TERENCE WEIL   *Continuo Bass:* ROBIN MCGEE

Harpsichords made by TOM GOFF *and* JACOBUS KIRKMAN

Organs built by HILL NORMAN & BEARD

Scenery built by THE RINGMER BUILDING WORKS LTD. *under the supervision of* R. W. GOUGH *and* S. ZEAL

Scenery painted by HARKER, HOMAN & BRAVERY LTD, *under the supervision of* CHARLES BRAVERY *and* DAVID HOMAN

Costumes made by the GLYNDEBOURNE OPERA WARDROBE, *and by* BONN & MACKENZIE LTD., *under the supervision of* ROSEMARY WILKINS

Wigs by WIG CREATIONS   *Shoes by* ANELLO & DAVIDE

Armour made by CONSTANCE OLDEN

Properties made at GLYNDEBOURNE *under the supervision of* HARRY KELLARD

Cast

Ottone, *Poppea's former lover*	Walter Alberti *(Italian)*
First Soldier	Dennis Brandt *(English)*
Second Soldier	Gerald English *(English)*
Poppea	Judith Raskin *(American)*
Nerone, *Emperor of Rome*	Richard Lewis *(English)*
Arnalta, *Poppea's old nurse*	{ Oralia Dominguez *(Mexican)* / *Jean Allister *(Irish)*
Ottavia, *the Empress*	Frances Bible *(American)*
Damigella, *in Ottavia's service*	Soo-Bee Lee *(Chinese)*
Seneca, *elder statesman and philosopher*	Carlo Cava *(Italian)*
Valetto, *in Ottavia's service*	Duncan Robertson *(Scottish)*
Drusilla, *a Court lady*	Lydia Marimpietri *(Italian)*
Pallade, *Goddess of Wisdom*	Josephine Allen *(English)*
Liberto, *Captain of the guard*	John Shirley-Quirk *(English)*
Lucano, *a friend of Nerone*	Hugues Cuenod *(Swiss)*
Amor, *God of Love*	Marta Sellas *(Scottish)*
A Lictor	Dennis Wicks *(English)*
The Emperor's Fool *(mute)*	Robert Harrold *(English)*

ACT I

DINNER INTERVAL OF APPROXIMATELY 75 MINUTES

ACT II

Dates of Performance: June 29 · July 1 · 7 · 11 · 13 · 15 · 24 · 28 · August 1 · 3* · 5* · 10*

The Audience is particularly requested to refrain from applauding until the music has stopped at the end of a scene or aria.

KARLHEINZ STOCKHAUSEN (Born 1928)

Punkte

London 14 January 1970	BBC SO	Unpublished radio broadcast

JOHANN STRAUSS I (1804-1849)

Explosionen, polka

London 14 August 1971	BBC SO	CD: Radio Classics BBCRD 9109

Radetzky March

London 12 August 1972	BBC SO	Unpublished radio broadcast

JOHANN STRAUSS II (1825-1899)

An der schönen blauen Donau, waltz

Walthamstow 8 December 1961	LPO	LP: Pye GGL 0127/GSGL 10127/MAL 571
London 12 August 1971	BBC SO	Unpublished radio broadcast

Banditengalop

London 12 August 1972	BBC SO	Unpublished radio broadcast

Die Fledermaus, excerpt (Klänge der Heimat)

London 12 August 1972	BBC SO C.Wilson	Unpublished radio broadcast

Freikugeln, polka

London 12 August 1972	BBC SO	Unpublished radio broadcast

Kaiserwalzer

Walthamstow 8 December 1961	LPO	LP: Pye GGL 0127/GSGL 10127/MAL 571
London 14 August 1971	BBC SO	CD: Radio Classics BBCRD 9109 <u>Also on Radio Classics sampler CD</u>

Perpetuum mobile

London   BBC SO   CD: Radio Classics BBCRD 9109
14 August
1971

London   BBC SO   Unpublished radio broadcast
12 August
1972

Ritter Pasman, Csardas

London   BBC SO   Unpublished radio broadcast
12 August
1972

Waldmeister, overture

London   LPO   Unpublished radio broadcast
24 August
1963

JOSEF STRAUSS (1827-1870)

Feuerfest, polka

London 12 August 1972	BBC SO	Unpublished radio broadcast

Mein Lebenslauf ist Lieb' und Lust, waltz

London 12 August 1972	BBC SO	Unpublished radio broadcast

Plappermäulchen, polka

London 12 August 1972	BBC SO	Unpublished radio broadcast

Sphärenklänge, waltz

London 14 August 1971	BBC SO	CD: Radio Classics BBCRD 9109

JOSEF AND JOHANN STRAUSS

Pizzicato polka

London 14 August 1971	BBC SO	CD: Radio Classics BBCRD 9109

RICHARD STRAUSS (1864-1949)

Ariadne auf Naxos

Glyndebourne 16 July 1954	RPO Amara, Dobbs, Jurinac, R.Lewis, G.Evans, Gester	Unpublished radio broadcast

Don Juan

London 28 August 1975	LSO	Unpublished radio broadcast
London 17 December 1982	BBC SO	CD: Radio Classics 15656 91572

Don Quixote

London 11 August 1976	BBC Philharmonic H.Schiff	Unpublished radio broadcast

Intermezzo

Glyndebourne 13 July 1974	LPO Glyndebourne Festival Chorus Söderström, Gale, Oliver, Bakker	Unpublished radio broadcast

Guntram

London 19 March 1981	BBC SO BBC Singers Farley, S.Walker, W.Lewis, Douglas, Tomlinson, Sharpe	Unpublished radio broadcast

Tod und Verklärung

London 10 January 1980	BBC SO	CD: Radio Classics BBCRD 9122

4 letzte Lieder

London 3 February 1972	BBC SO Kanawa	Unpublished radio broadcast

Der Rosenkavalier

Glyndebourne 14 August 1965	LPO Caballé, Hammes, Zylis-Gara, Andrew, Edelmann, Modenos	LP: Historical Recording Enterprises HRE 356 Abridged recording

IGOR STRAVINSKY (1882-1971)

Concerto for 2 pianos and orchestra

London 14 August 1968	LPO Ogdon, Lucas	Unpublished radio broadcast

Violin Concerto

Cheltenham 6 July 1973	BBC SO Marschner	Unpublished radio broadcast

L'histoire du soldat

London 12 April- 25 May 1955	RPO Helpmann, Langdon, Nicholls	LP: HMV ALP 1377/HQM 1008 LP: Victor LM 2079 Excerpt LP: HMV HMS 109

L'oiseau de feu, 1919 suite

Barking 16-18 June 1969	LPO	LP: Pye TPLS 13032/GSGC 15002

KAREL SZYMANOWSKI (1882-1937)

Harnasie, ballet pantomime

London 17 March 1987	BBC SO BBC Chorus Friend	Unpublished radio broadcast

PIOTR TCHAIKOVSKY (1840-1893)

Piano Concerto No 1

Barking 7-8 April 1970	LPO Katin	LP: EMI CFP 115

Evgeny Onegin

London 11 August 1970	LPO Glyndebourne Festival Chorus Söderström, Milchewa, Bowden, Ochman, Cuenod, Vassilev	Unpublished radio broadcast

Romeo and Juliet, fantasy overture

Barking 7-8 April 1970	LPO	LP: EMI CFP 106/CFP 40042/CFP 40307/ CFP 40319

Romeo and Juliet, duet for soprano, tenor and orchestra

Edinburgh August 1961	LSO Collier, R.Lewis	Unpublished radio broadcast

AMBROISE THOMAS (1811-1896)

Mignon, excerpt (Connais-tu le pays?)

London 4-10 January 1976	LPO Stade	LP: CBS 76522 CD: Sony 39315

MICHAEL TIPPETT (Born 1905)

A Child of our time

Liverpool 17-19 March 1957	Liverpool PO and Chorus Morison, Bowden, R.Lewis, Standen	LP: Pye CCL 30114-30115 LP: Decca DA 19-20/ZDA 19-20/ DPA 571-572 CD: Decca 425 1582/461 1232

King Priam

Coventry 29 May 1962	Covent Garden Orchestra & Chorus Collier, Elkins, R.Lewis, Dobson, Ward	Unpublished radio broadcast <u>World premiere performance</u>

The Midsummer Marriage, Ritual dances

London 27-31 October 1957	Covent Garden Orchestra	LP: Pye CCL 30114-30115 LP: Decca DA 19-20/ZDA 19-20/ DPA 571-572

GIUSEPPE VERDI (1813-1901)

Aida, excerpts

Walthamstow 25-28 April 1963	Covent Garden Orchestra Nilsson, G.Hoffman, Ottolini, L.Quilico	LP: Decca LXT 6068/SXL 6068 <u>Ritorna vincitor</u> LP: Decca 411 8851

Don Carlo, excerpt (Tu che la vanità)

London 17-21 September 1981	LPO Kanawa	LP: CBS 37298 CD: Sony 37298

Falstaff

Glyndebourne August 1976	LPO Glyndebourne Festival Chorus Griffel, Gale, Penkova, Condò, Cosotti, Gramm, Luxon	VHS Video: Longman LGVH 7014 VHS Video: Pickwick SLL 7014

La forza del destino, excerpt (Pace pace, mio Dio!)

London 24 February- 4 December 1976	New Philharmonia Cotrubas	LP: CBS 76521

Macbeth

Glyndebourne August 1972	LPO Glyndebourne Festival Chorus Barstow, Erwen, Paskalis, Morris	VHS Video: Longman LGVH 7017/LGBE 7017/ Pickwick SLL 7017

Rigoletto, excerpt (Caro nome)

London 24 February- 4 December 1976	New Philharmonia Cotrubas	LP: CBS 76521

La traviata

Florence 7-16 November 1962	Maggio musicale Orchestra & Chorus Sutherland, Bergonzi, Merrill	LP: Decca MET 249-251/SET 249-251 CD: Decca 411 8772 Excerpts LP: Decca LXT 6127/SXL 6127 CD: Decca 440 4172
New York 4 February 1984	Metropolitan Opera Orchestra & Chorus Andrade, Raffanti, Sereni	Unpublished Met broadcast

La traviata, excerpt (E strano!/Sempre libera!)

London 17-21 September 1981	LPO Kanawa	LP: CBS 37298 CD: Sony 37298

Il trovatore, excerpt (D'amor sull'ali rosee)

London 17-21 September 1981	LPO Kanawa	LP: CBS 37298 CD: Sony 37298

WILLIAM WALTON (1902-1983)

Symphony No 2

Edinburgh 2 September 1960	Liverpool PO	Unpublished radio broadcast World premiere performance

Belshazzar's Feast

London 20 July 1984	BBC SO BBC Chorus LPO Choir Roberts	CD: Radio Classics 15656 91612

CARL MARIA VON WEBER (1786-1826)

Der Freischütz, excerpt (Leise leise)

London 12-15 November 1987	Philharmonia Mattila	LP: Philips 422 0731 CD: Philips 422 0732

MALCOLM WILLIAMSON (Born 1931)

Hammarskjöld Portrait

London 30 July 1974	BBC SO Söderström	Unpublished radio broadcast World premiere performance

ERMANNO WOLF-FERRARI (1876-1948)

Il segreto di Susanna

London 3-9 August 1980	Philharmonia Scotto, Bruson	LP: CBS 40134 CD: Sony 36733

CHRISTMAS CAROLS

O come all ye faithful

London 3 October 1952	Philharmonia Covent Garden and Hampstead Choirs Schwarzkopf	Columbia unpublished

The first Nowell

London 3 October 1952	Philharmonia Covent Garden and Hampstead Choirs Schwarzkopf	78: Columbia LB 131 45: Columbia SCD 2112 LP: Legendary LR 136

Stille Nacht, heilige Nacht

London 3 October 1952	Philharmonia Covent Garden and Hampstead Choirs Schwarzkopf <u>Sung in English</u>	78: Columbia LB 131 45: Columbia SCD 2112

BRITISH FOLKSONGS

An Eriskay love lilt

Vienna 9-13 April 1954	M.Dickie Pritchard, piano	LP: Philips NBR 6016

Believe me if all those endearing young charms

Vienna 9-13 April 1954	M.Dickie Pritchard, piano	45: Philips NBE 11070 LP: Philips NBR 6016

Bonnie Mary of Argyll

Vienna 9-13 April 1954	M.Dickie Pritchard, piano	45: Philips NBE 11070 LP: Philips NBR 6016

Drink to me only

Vienna 9-13 April 1954	M.Dickie Pritchard, piano	45: Philips NBE 11070 LP: Philips NBR 6016

Kishmul's Galley

Vienna 9-13 April 1954	M.Dickie Pritchard, piano	LP: Philips NBR 6016

Kitty of Coleraine

Vienna 9-13 April 1954	M.Dickie Pritchard, piano	LP: Philips NBR 6016

Land of heart's desire

Vienna   M.Dickie   LP: Philips NBR 6016
9-13   Pritchard, piano
April
1954

My Lady Greensleeves

Vienna   M.Dickie   LP: Philips NBR 6016
9-13   Pritchard, piano
April
1954

My love is like a red red rose

Vienna   M.Dickie   45: Philips NBE 11070
9-13   Pritchard, piano   LP: Philips NBR 6016
April
1954

The plough boy

Vienna   M.Dickie   45: Philips NBE 11070
9-13   Pritchard, piano   LP: Philips NBR 6016
April
1954

The star of the County Down

Vienna   M.Dickie   LP: Philips NBR 6016
9-13   Pritchard, piano
April
1954

Think on me

Vienna   M.Dickie   LP: Philips NBR 6016
9-13   Pritchard, piano
April
1954

PRITCHARD'S SPEECH AT THE LAST NIGHT OF THE PROMS

London
16 September
1989

CD: BBC PC98 SE

Discographies

Teachers and pupils
Schwarzkopf / Ivogün / Cebotari /
Seinemeyer / Welitsch / Streich / Berger
7 separate discographies, 400 pages

The post-war German tradition
Kempe / Keilberth / Sawallisch / Kubelik /
Cluytens
5 separate discographies, 300 pages

**Mid-century conductors
and More Viennese singers**
Böhm / De Sabata / Knappertsbusch / Serafin /
Krauss / Dermota / Rysanek / Wächter /
Reining / Kunz
10 separate discographies, 420 pages

Leopold Stokowski
Discography and concert register, 300 pages

Tenors in a lyric tradition
Fritz Wunderlich / Walther Ludwig /
Peter Anders
3 separate discographies, 350 pages

Makers of the Philharmonia
Galliera / Susskind / Kletzki / Malko / Matacic /
Dobrowen / Kurtz / Fistoulari
8 separate discographies, 300 pages

A notable quartet
Janowitz / Ludwig / Gedda / Fischer-Dieskau
4 separate discographies, 600 pages

Hungarians in exile
Reiner / Dorati / Szell
3 separate discographies, 300 pages

The art of the diva
Muzio / Callas / Olivero
3 separate discographies, 225 pages

The lyric baritone
Reinmar / Hüsch / Metternich / Uhde /
Wächter
5 separate discographies, 225 pages

Price £22 per volume (£28 outside UK)
*Special offer any 3 volumes for
£55 (£75 outside UK)*
Postage included
Order from: John Hunt, Flat 6,
37 Chester Way, London SE11 4UR

Credits

Valuable help with the supply of
information or illustration material
for these discographies came from

Stathis Arfanis, Athens
Christopher Dyment, Welwyn
Richard Chlupaty, London
Clifford Elkin, Glasgow
Bill Flowers, London
Michael Gray, Alexandria VA
Syd Gray, Hove
Bill Holland, Polygram London
Ken Jagger, EMI Classics London
Raymond Klumper-Horneman, London
Roderick Krüsemann, Amsterdam
Johan Maarsingh, Utrecht
Nico Steffen, Huizen
Ronald Taylor, Barnet
Malcolm Walker, Harrow

Music and Books published by Travis & Emery Music Bookshop:

Anon.: Hymnarium Sarisburiense, cum Rubricis et Notis Musicis.
Agricola, Johann Friedrich from Tosi: Anleitung zur Singkunst.
Bach, C.P.E.: edited W. Emery: Nekrolog or Obituary Notice of J.S. Bach.
Bateson, Naomi Judith: Alcock of Salisbury
Bathe, William: A Briefe Introduction to the Skill of Song (c.1587)
Bax, Arnold: Symphony #5, Arranged for Piano Four Hands by Walter Emery
Burney, Charles: The Present State of Music in France and Italy (1771)
Burney, Charles: The Present State of Music in Germany, Netherlands... (1773)
Burney, Charles: An Account of the Musical Performances ... Handel (1784)
Burney, Karl: Nachricht von Georg Friedrich Handel's Lebensumstanden (1784)
Burns, Robert: The Caledonian Musical Museum ... Best Scotch Songs (1810)
Cobbett, W.W.: Cobbett's Cyclopedic Survey of Chamber Music. (2 vols.)
Corrette, Michel: Le Maitre de Clavecin (1753)
Crimp, Bryan: Dear Mr. Rosenthal ... Dear Mr. Gaisberg ...
Crimp, Bryan: Solo: The Biography of Solomon
d'Indy, Vincent: Beethoven: Biographie Critique (in French, 1911)
d'Indy, Vincent: Beethoven: A Critical Biography (in English, 1912)
d'Indy, Vincent: César Franck (in French, 1910)
Fischhof, Joseph: Versuch einer Geschichte des Clavierbaues (1853).
Frescobaldi, Girolamo: D'Arie Musicali per Cantarsi. Primo & Secondo Libro.
Geminiani, Francesco: The Art of Playing the Violin (1751)
Handel; Purcell; Boyce et al: Calliope or English Harmony: Vol. First. (1746)
Häuser: Musikalisches Lexikon. 2 vols in one.
Hawkins, John: General History of the Science & Practice of Music (5 vols. 1776)
Herbert-Caesari, Edgar: The Science and Sensations of Vocal Tone
Herbert-Caesari, Edgar: Vocal Truth
Hopkins and Rimboult: The Organ. Its History and Construction.
Hunt, John: Adam to Webern: the recordings of von Karajan
Hunt, John: several discographies – see separate list.
Isaacs, Lewis: Hänsel and Gretel. A Guide to Humperdinck's Opera.
Isaacs, Lewis: Königskinder (Royal Children) A Guide to Humperdinck's Opera.
Kastner: Manuel Général de Musique Militaire
Lacassagne, M. l'Abbé Joseph : Traité Général des élémens du Chant.
Lascelles (née Catley), Anne: The Life of Miss Anne Catley.
Mainwaring, John: Memoirs of the Life of the Late George Frederic Handel
Malcolm, Alexander: A Treaty of Music: Speculative, Practical and Historical
Marx, Adolph Bernhard: Die Kunst des Gesanges, Theoretisch-Practisch (1826)
May, Florence: The Life of Brahms (2nd edition)
May, Florence: The Girlhood Of Clara Schumann: Clara Wieck And Her Time.
Mellers, Wilfrid: Angels of the Night: Popular Female Singers of Our Time
Mellers, Wilfrid: Bach and the Dance of God
Mellers, Wilfrid: Beethoven and the Voice of God
Mellers, Wilfrid: Caliban Reborn - Renewal in Twentieth Century Music

Music and Books published by Travis & Emery Music Bookshop:

Mellers, Wilfrid: François Couperin and the French Classical Tradition
Mellers, Wilfrid: Harmonious Meeting
Mellers, Wilfrid: Le Jardin Retrouvé, The Music of Frederic Mompou
Mellers, Wilfrid: Music and Society, England and the European Tradition
Mellers, Wilfrid: Music in a New Found Land: ... ... American Music
Mellers, Wilfrid: Romanticism and the Twentieth Century (from 1800)
Mellers, Wilfrid: The Masks of Orpheus: ...... the Story of European Music.
Mellers, Wilfrid: The Sonata Principle (from c. 1750)
Mellers, Wilfrid: Vaughan Williams and the Vision of Albion
Panchianio, Cattuffio: Rutzvanscad Il Giovine (1737)
Pearce, Charles: Sims Reeves, Fifty Years of Music in England.
Pettitt, Stephen: Philharmonia Orchestra: Complete Discography (1987)
Playford, John: An Introduction to the Skill of Musick (1674)
Purcell, Henry et al: Harmonia Sacra ... The First Book, (1726)
Purcell, Henry et al: Harmonia Sacra ... Book II (1726)
Quantz, Johann: Versuch einer Anweisung die Flöte traversiere zu spielen.
Rameau, Jean-Philippe: Code de Musique Pratique, ou Methodes (1760)
Rastall, Richard: The Notation of Western Music.
Rimbault, Edward: The Pianoforte, Its Origins, Progress, and Construction.
Rousseau, Jean Jacques: Dictionnaire de Musique
Rubinstein, Anton : Guide to the proper use of the Pianoforte Pedals.
Sainsbury, John S.: Dictionary of Musicians. Vol. 1. (1825). 2 vols.
Serré de Rieux, Jean de : Les dons des Enfans de Latone
Simpson, Christopher: A Compendium of Practical Musick in Five Parts
Spohr, Louis: Autobiography
Spohr, Louis: Grand Violin School
Tans'ur, William: A New Musical Grammar; or The Harmonical Spectator
Terry, Charles Sanford: John Christian Bach (Johann Christian Bach) (1929)
Terry, Charles Sanford: J.S. Bach's Original Hymn-Tunes for Congregational Use
Terry, Charles Sanford: Four-Part Chorals of J.S. Bach. (German & English)
Terry, Charles Sanford: Joh. Seb. Bach, Cantata Texts, Sacred and Secular.
Terry, Charles Sanford: The Origins of the Family of Bach Musicians.
Tosi, Pierfrancesco: Opinioni de' Cantori Antichi, e Moderni (1723)
Van der Straeten, Edmund: History of the Violoncello, The Viol da Gamba ...
Van der Straeten, Edmund: History of the Violin, Its Ancestors... (2 vols.)
Waltern: Musikalisches Lexicon
Walther, J. G.: Musicalisches Lexikon ober Musicalische Bibliothec

Travis & Emery Music Bookshop
17 Cecil Court, London, WC2N 4EZ, United Kingdom.
Tel. (+44) 20 7240 2129

© Travis & Emery 2009

Discographies by Travis & Emery:
Discographies by John Hunt.

1987: 978-1-906857-14-1: From Adam to Webern: the Recordings of von Karajan.
1991: 978-0-951026-83-0: 3 Italian Conductors and 7 Viennese Sopranos: 10 Discographies: Arturo Toscanini, Guido Cantelli, Carlo Maria Giulini, Elisabeth Schwarzkopf, Irmgard Seefried, Elisabeth Gruemmer, Sena Jurinac, Hilde Gueden, Lisa Della Casa, Rita Streich.
1992: 978-0-951026-85-4: Mid-Century Conductors and More Viennese Singers: 10 Discographies: Karl Boehm, Victor De Sabata, Hans Knappertsbusch, Tullio Serafin, Clemens Krauss, Anton Dermota, Leonie Rysanek, Eberhard Waechter, Maria Reining, Erich Kunz.
1993: 978-0-951026-87-8: More 20th Century Conductors: 7 Discographies: Eugen Jochum, Ferenc Fricsay, Carl Schuricht, Felix Weingartner, Josef Krips, Otto Klemperer, Erich Kleiber.
1994: 978-0-951026-88-5: Giants of the Keyboard: 6 Discographies: Wilhelm Kempff, Walter Gieseking, Edwin Fischer, Clara Haskil, Wilhelm Backhaus, Artur Schnabel.
1994: 978-0-951026-89-2: Six Wagnerian Sopranos: 6 Discographies: Frieda Leider, Kirsten Flagstad, Astrid Varnay, Martha Moedl, Birgit Nilsson, Gwyneth Jones.
1995: 978-0-952582-70-0: Musical Knights: 6 Discographies: Henry Wood, Thomas Beecham, Adrian Boult, John Barbirolli, Reginald Goodall, Malcolm Sargent.
1995: 978-0-952582-71-7: A Notable Quartet: 4 Discographies: Gundula Janowitz, Christa Ludwig, Nicolai Gedda, Dietrich Fischer-Dieskau.
1996: 978-0-952582-72-4: The Post-War German Tradition: 5 Discographies: Rudolf Kempe, Joseph Keilberth, Wolfgang Sawallisch, Rafael Kubelik, Andre Cluytens.
1996: 978-0-952582-73-1: Teachers and Pupils: 7 Discographies: Elisabeth Schwarzkopf, Maria Ivoguen, Maria Cebotari, Meta Seinemeyer, Ljuba Welitsch, Rita Streich, Erna Berger.
1996: 978-0-952582-77-9: Tenors in a Lyric Tradition: 3 Discographies: Peter Anders, Walther Ludwig, Fritz Wunderlich.
1997: 978-0-952582-78-6: The Lyric Baritone: 5 Discographies: Hans Reinmar, Gerhard Huesch, Josef Metternich, Hermann Uhde, Eberhard Waechter.
1997: 978-0-952582-79-3: Hungarians in Exile: 3 Discographies: Fritz Reiner, Antal Dorati, George Szell.
1997: 978-1-901395-00-6: The Art of the Diva: 3 Discographies: Claudia Muzio, Maria Callas, Magda Olivero.
1997: 978-1-901395-01-3: Metropolitan Sopranos: 4 Discographies: Rosa Ponselle, Eleanor Steber, Zinka Milanov, Leontyne Price.
1997: 978-1-901395-02-0: Back From The Shadows: 4 Discographies: Willem Mengelberg, Dimitri Mitropoulos, Hermann Abendroth, Eduard Van Beinum.
1997: 978-1-901395-03-7: More Musical Knights: 4 Discographies: Hamilton Harty, Charles Mackerras, Simon Rattle, John Pritchard.
1998: 978-1-901395-94-5: Conductors On The Yellow Label: 8 Discographies: Fritz Lehmann, Ferdinand Leitner, Ferenc Fricsay, Eugen Jochum, Leopold Ludwig, Artur Rother, Franz Konwitschny, Igor Markevitch.
1998: 978-1-901395-95-2: More Giants of the Keyboard: 5 Discographies: Claudio Arrau, Gyorgy Cziffra, Vladimir Horowitz, Dinu Lipatti, Artur Rubinstein.
1998: 978-1-901395-96-9: Mezzo and Contraltos: 5 Discographies: Janet Baker, Margarete Klose, Kathleen Ferrier, Giulietta Simionato, Elisabeth Hoengen.

1999: 978-1-901395-97-6: The Furtwaengler Sound Sixth Edition: Discography and Concert Listing.
1999: 978-1-901395-98-3: The Great Dictators: 3 Discographies: Evgeny Mravinsky, Artur Rodzinski, Sergiu Celibidache.
1999: 978-1-901395-99-0: Sviatoslav Richter: Pianist of the Century: Discography.
2000: 978-1-901395-04-4: Philharmonic Autocrat 1: Discography of: Herbert Von Karajan [Third Edition].
2000: 978-1-901395-05-1: Wiener Philharmoniker 1 - Vienna Philharmonic and Vienna State Opera Orchestras: Discography Part 1 1905-1954.
2000: 978-1-901395-06-8: Wiener Philharmoniker 2 - Vienna Philharmonic and Vienna State Opera Orchestras: Discography Part 2 1954-1989.
2001: 978-1-901395-07-5: Gramophone Stalwarts: 3 Separate Discographies: Bruno Walter, Erich Leinsdorf, Georg Solti.
2001: 978-1-901395-08-2: Singers of the Third Reich: 5 Discographies: Helge Roswaenge, Tiana Lemnitz, Franz Voelker, Maria Mueller, Max Lorenz.
2001: 978-1-901395-09-9: Philharmonic Autocrat 2: Concert Register of Herbert Von Karajan Second Edition.
2002: 978-1-901395-10-5: Sächsische Staatskapelle Dresden: Complete Discography.
2002: 978-1-901395-11-2: Carlo Maria Giulini: Discography and Concert Register.
2002: 978-1-901395-12-9: Pianists For The Connoisseur: 6 Discographies: Arturo Benedetti Michelangeli, Alfred Cortot, Alexis Weissenberg, Clifford Curzon, Solomon, Elly Ney.
2003: 978-1-901395-14-3: Singers on the Yellow Label: 7 Discographies: Maria Stader, Elfriede Troetschel, Annelies Kupper, Wolfgang Windgassen, Ernst Haefliger, Josef Greindl, Kim Borg.
2003: 978-1-901395-15-0: A Gallic Trio: 3 Discographies: Charles Muench, Paul Paray, Pierre Monteux.
2004: 978-1-901395-16-7: Antal Dorati 1906-1988: Discography and Concert Register.
2004: 978-1-901395-17-4: Columbia 33CX Label Discography.
2004: 978-1-901395-18-1: Great Violinists: 3 Discographies: David Oistrakh, Wolfgang Schneiderhan, Arthur Grumiaux.
2006: 978-1-901395-19-8: Leopold Stokowski: Second Edition of the Discography.
2006: 978-1-901395-20-4: Wagner Im Festspielhaus: Discography of the Bayreuth Festival.
2006: 978-1-901395-21-1: Her Master's Voice: Concert Register and Discography of Dame Elisabeth Schwarzkopf [Third Edition].
2007: 978-1-901395-22-8: Hans Knappertsbusch: Kna: Concert Register and Discography of Hans Knappertsbusch, 1888-1965. Second Edition.
2008: 978-1-901395-23-5: Philips Minigroove: Second Extended Version of the European Discography.
2009: 978-1-901395--24-2: American Classics: The Discographies of Leonard Bernstein and Eugene Ormandy.

Discography by Stephen J. Pettitt, edited by John Hunt:
1987: 978-1-906857-16-5: Philharmonia Orchestra: Complete Discography 1945-1987

Available from: Travis & Emery at 17 Cecil Court, London, UK. (+44) 20 7 240 2129. email on sales@travis-and-emery.com .

© Travis & Emery 2009

www.ingramcontent.com/pod-product-compliance
Lightning Source LLC
Chambersburg PA
CBHW052049230426
43671CB00011B/1849